JEREMIAH
BIBLE STUDY SERIES

REVELATION

THE ULTIMATE HOPE IN CHRIST

DR. DAVID JEREMIAH

Prepared by Peachtree Publishing Services

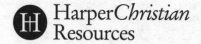

Harper*Christian*
Resources

REVELATION
JEREMIAH BIBLE STUDY SERIES

© 2022 by Dr. David Jeremiah

Requests for information should be addressed to:
HarperChristian Resources, 3900 Sparks Dr. SE, Grand Rapids, Michigan 49546

ISBN 978-0-310-09186-8 (softcover)
ISBN 978-0-310-09187-5 (ebook)

HarperChristian Resources titles may be purchased in bulk for church, business, fundraising,
or ministry use. For information, please email ResourceSpecialist@ChurchSource.com.

Produced with the assistance of Peachtree Publishing Services (www.PeachtreePublishingServices.
com). Project staff includes Christopher D. Hudson and Randy Southern.

First Printing July 2022 / Printed in the United States of America

23 24 25 26 27 LBC 10 9 8 7 6

CONTENTS

INTRODUCTION TO
The Revelation of Jesus Christ

"I saw under the altar the souls of those who had been slain for the word of God and for the testimony which they held. And they cried with a loud voice, saying, 'How long, O Lord, holy and true, until You judge and avenge our blood on those who dwell on the earth?" (Revelation 6:9–10). This question has been the cry of believers for more than two millennia. How long will godly people have to suffer while evil prevails? How long must we continue to endure in this fallen world? How long will Jesus' return be delayed? The answer that God provides to the apostle John through the book of Revelation reveals both His sovereignty and His grace: *until the plan of salvation has been accomplished.* Throughout the book, we see the tension play out between judgment and redemption, with God several times pausing his acts to issue a call to repentance. For all its prophetic value, the book of Revelation is also a stunning testament to God's faithfulness—and a plea for all people to receive the grace and mercy that He offers while there is still time.

AUTHOR AND DATE

The author of Revelation identifies himself as "John, who bore witness to . . . the testimony of Jesus Christ" (1:1–2), and his words reveal that he was well acquainted with the persecution being inflicted on believers in Asia Minor. Early church fathers such as Justin Martyr (c. AD 100–165), Irenaeus (c. 130–202), and Clement of Alexandria (c. 150–212) all pointed to the disciple John as the author. This position was not challenged until the third century, when Dionysius of Alexandria identified dissimilarities between Revelation and John's other writings and concluded the book could not have been written by the same person. Dionysius instead pointed to a first-century Christian leader named John the Presbyter as the author. Despite his conclusions, many scholars today point to the disciple John as the author. Early church tradition held that John was exiled to the isle of Patmos (see 1:9) during the reign of the Roman emperor Domitian, which would place the writing around AD 95.

BACKGROUND AND SETTING

John addresses his work to seven churches in Asia Minor—Ephesus, Smyrna, Pergamos, Thyatira, Sardis, Philadelphia, and Laodicea—who were facing persecution and being tempted to revert to their old ways of life. In particular, Roman authorities at the end of the first century were enforcing emperor worship as a means of testing a community's loyalty, and Christians were being pressured to compromise to this practice in violation of their beliefs. John's words thus serve as a warning to *these* believers to stay true to Christ . . . while at the same time instructing *all* believers of the prophetic events to come when He returns to judge the world. Revelation is thus a reminder to believers in every age that Jesus is Lord of all, that He will one day destroy the devil, and that those who remain faithful to Him in this life—no matter what they face—will be able to join in His triumph and receive the rewards of eternal life.

KEY THEMES

Several key themes are prominent in the book of Revelation. The first is that *believers in Christ must never compromise.* Tucked inside the book of Revelation are seven letters, given by Jesus to John, to seven churches located in Asia Minor. In each letter, Jesus reveals His knowledge of each church's works, its strengths and weaknesses, and its victories and challenges. He empathizes with His people's suffering but demands they remain faithful to Him. He knows of what they are capable and will not settle for anything less (see 2:1–3:22; 13:1–18; 17:1–18:24).

A second theme is that *believers in Christ can rely on God's promises of deliverance.* Early in the book of Revelation, Jesus tells one faithful group of believers, "Because you have kept My command to persevere, I also will keep you from the hour of trial which shall come upon the whole world" (3:10). This promise from Christ—and the absence of the church throughout the central chapters of Revelation—affirm that God will deliver His church from the trials of the Tribulation that will inflict the earth in the last days. The destiny of all followers of Christ who persevere is to *reign* with Him, not be punished by Him (see 19:1–10; 20:1–6).

A third theme is that *believers in Christ can be assured that evil will not triumph.* Satan and his forces repeatedly wage war against the authority of God throughout the book of Revelation and attempt to lead the world astray. However, in the end, we find that it is *God* who will secure the ultimate victory. Jesus, the Lamb who was slain for the sins of the world, will put down all rebellions against God and reign victorious. Satan will finally be defeated and forever punished for his wickedness (see 1:5; 5:5–10; 12:1–11; 17:14; 19:16; 20:7–10).

A fourth theme is that *believers in Christ should worship God for His gift of salvation.* The book of Revelation reveals that God has made His offer of salvation available to anyone who accepts the sacrifice for sins that Jesus made on the cross. Eternal victory belongs to Christ and *all* who place their hope in Him. The proper response to these acts of grace—as demonstrated throughout the book of Revelation by the heavenly host—is praise and worship to God. The people of God must be a worshiping people (see 4:1–5:14; 21:1–22:6).

KEY APPLICATIONS

The Book of Revelation provides hope to all faithful followers of Christ. While in this world we will face pain, suffering, and persecution, these trials are only temporary. Evil may be having its way in the *present*, but righteousness will have its way for all *eternity*. Jesus will be victorious over Satan. Sorrow, sickness, sin, and death will disappear. A new heaven and new earth will emerge from the ashes of the old. God will wipe away the tear from every eye. We are assured of this happy ending to our story . . . and nothing on earth, heaven, or hell can ever take it away. So, when the heartaches of this world weigh us down, we only need to look up and look ahead to the incredible and eternal future that God has in store for us.

A VISION IN EXILE

Revelation 1:1–20

GETTING STARTED

What image of Jesus do you get from reading the Gospels?

_____

_____

_____

_____

_____

_____

_____

_____

_____

_____

_____

_____

_____

_____

_____

SETTING THE STAGE

Jesus chose twelve men to be His disciples during His time of ministry on earth. But of those twelve, only Peter, James, and John comprised what we might call His "inner circle." These men were present with Him during special events such as the raising of Jairus's daughter (see Luke 8:49–56), the Transfiguration (see Mark 9:2–3), and His time of prayer in the Garden of Gethsemane (see Matthew 26:36–38). They were His closest friends.

Jesus' bond with John was so strong that on the cross, He entrusted the care of His mother to him (see John 19:26–27). John ultimately became a "pillar" in the early church (see Galatians 2:9) and likely ministered in the city of Ephesus. But sometime around AD 95, he was exiled by the Roman authorities to the island of Patmos in the Aegean Sea for the "crime" of preaching the gospel. John's banishment allowed him to escape the death sentence, but his exile would have constituted a miserable existence marked by chains, forced labor, and a lack of basic necessities.

In the midst of this dark setting, the Word of God comes to John and the glory of the risen Christ is revealed to him. As John describes the scene, he is "in the Spirit on the Lord's Day" (Revelation 1:10) when he receives a vision. He is allowed to move "upward" to see events taking place in heaven and "forward" to see things that will occur in the future. This happens on "the Lord's Day," which could refer to the "Day of the Lord," a designation for the time when God will bring human history to a climax through a series of cataclysmic events.

The vision that John witnessed must have startled him. Despite the number of years that had passed since he had last seen Jesus, he would have certainly still had vivid memories of Jesus' earthly appearance. But the One he saw in his vision bore little resemblance to the man he had known. This Christ was not the lowly Galilean rabbi or the gentle Lamb of God. He was the awe-inspiring Judge of the nations revealed in all His glory—the mighty Lion of God.

EXPLORING THE TEXT

Introduction and Benediction (Revelation 1:1–5)

---

¹ The Revelation of Jesus Christ, which God gave Him to show His servants—things which must shortly take place. And He sent and

signified it by His angel to His servant John, ² who bore witness to the word of God, and to the testimony of Jesus Christ, to all things that he saw. ³ Blessed is he who reads and those who hear the words of this prophecy, and keep those things which are written in it; for the time is near.

⁴ John, to the seven churches which are in Asia:

Grace to you and peace from Him who is and who was and who is to come, and from the seven Spirits who are before His throne, ⁵ and from Jesus Christ, the faithful witness, the firstborn from the dead, and the ruler over the kings of the earth.

---

1. John begins by describing the nature of the prophetic book that he has written. He states that the events he will describe will "shortly" take place, which in his day was simply a way of saying that they could happen at *any time*. How does John describe himself as the author? Who does he say will be blessed by his words (see verses 1–3)?

_____

_____

_____

_____

2. John writes that his words are intended for the members of seven churches located in the Roman province of Asia (modern-day Turkey). He greets these readers with the phrase "grace to you and peace," which is typical of the greeting found in most of the New Testament epistles. Who does John say is the source of this grace and peace that they receive (see verses 4–5)?

_____

_____

_____

_____

_____

Greetings to the Seven Churches (Revelation 1:5–8)

⁵ To Him who loved us and washed us from our sins in His own blood, ⁶ and has made us kings and priests to His God and Father, to Him be glory and dominion forever and ever. Amen.

⁷ Behold, He is coming with clouds, and every eye will see Him, even they who pierced Him. And all the tribes of the earth will mourn because of Him. Even so, Amen.

⁸ "I am the Alpha and the Omega, the Beginning and the End," says the Lord, "who is and who was and who is to come, the Almighty."

3. Before John reveals the vision, he dedicates the book to his Savior. What acts of Christ does he single out in his dedication? What does he assure the believers will one day happen (see verses 5–7)?

4. John writes that Jesus identifies Himself as "the Alpha and the Omega," which are the first and last letters of the Greek alphabet, to announce that He is the Beginning and End (see verse 8). How does that description apply to His eternal nature and to His authority?

A Vision of the Son of Man (Revelation 1:9–16)

⁹ I, John, both your brother and companion in the tribulation and kingdom and patience of Jesus Christ, was on the island that is called

Patmos for the word of God and for the testimony of Jesus Christ. [10] I was in the Spirit on the Lord's Day, and I heard behind me a loud voice, as of a trumpet, [11] saying, "I am the Alpha and the Omega, the First and the Last," and, "What you see, write in a book and send it to the seven churches which are in Asia: to Ephesus, to Smyrna, to Pergamos, to Thyatira, to Sardis, to Philadelphia, and to Laodicea."

[12] Then I turned to see the voice that spoke with me. And having turned I saw seven golden lampstands, [13] and in the midst of the seven lampstands One like the Son of Man, clothed with a garment down to the feet and girded about the chest with a golden band. [14] His head and hair were white like wool, as white as snow, and His eyes like a flame of fire; [15] His feet were like fine brass, as if refined in a furnace, and His voice as the sound of many waters; [16] He had in His right hand seven stars, out of His mouth went a sharp two-edged sword, and His countenance was like the sun shining in its strength.

---

5. John reminds his readers that he is their "brother and companion" in the trials they are facing for Christ and that even in exile he is still serving his Lord. How does he describe the voice he heard in his vision? What instructions was he given (see verses 9–11)?

_____

_____

_____

_____

_____

_____

6. When John turns to look at the speaker, he sees a glorious figure wearing a long robe and girded with a golden band, both of which are symbolic of the garments worn by the priests in the Old Testament (see Daniel 10:5). What is the significance of this description? What else is unusual in John's description of Jesus' appearance (see Revelation 1:12–16)?

_____

_____

_____

_____

The First and the Last (Revelation 1:17–20)

> [17] And when I saw Him, I fell at His feet as dead. But He laid His right hand on me, saying to me, "Do not be afraid; I am the First and the Last. [18] I am He who lives, and was dead, and behold, I am alive forevermore. Amen. And I have the keys of Hades and of Death. [19] Write the things which you have seen, and the things which are, and the things which will take place after this. [20] The mystery of the seven stars which you saw in My right hand, and the seven golden lampstands: The seven stars are the angels of the seven churches, and the seven lampstands which you saw are the seven churches."

7. Jesus appears to John like "the sun shining in its strength" (verse 16), which simply means He reveals Himself in all His divine glory. How does John react? What words of assurance does Jesus give to John to identify Himself as his Lord (see verses 17–18)?

_____

_____

_____

_____

8. Jesus continues by instructing John to write down everything he is about to witness and then reveals the "mystery" of the seven stars and lampstands in the vision. What do the stars represent? What do the lampstands represent (see verses 19–20)?

_____

_____

_____

_____

REVIEWING THE STORY

John opens the book of Revelation with an explanation to his audience—believers located in seven churches in Asia Minor—that what they are about to read was revealed to him directly by Christ. He affirms that he is John the disciple, their brother and companion in tribulation, who is living in exile on the isle of Patmos. Following his opening greeting, he begins to relate a vision of a figure who is at once familiar and unrecognizable. The man is Jesus—whom he knew as the humble rabbi from Nazareth—revealed in all His glory. Jesus reveals Himself as the Alpha and Omega, the Beginning and the End, and the First and the Last. He instructs John to write down everything he is about to see for the benefit of the seven churches.

9. Why did God give this "revelation" or "vision" to John (see Revelation 1:1)?

_____

_____

_____

10. What has God done for all who choose to follow Christ (see Revelation 1:5–6)?

_____

_____

_____

11. How did Jesus announce Himself to John (see Revelation 1:10–11)?

_____

_____

_____

12. Why do Jesus' followers have no reason to fear His coming (see Revelation 1:17–18)?

_____

_____

_____

APPLYING THE MESSAGE

13. How does John's vision of Christ in all His glory affect your view of the Lord?

_____

_____

_____

14. What comfort can you take from knowing that you will one day share in Christ's glory?

_____

_____

_____

REFLECTING ON THE MEANING

In the opening chapter of Revelation, the disciple John records his vision of the glorified, risen, and majestic Jesus Christ. While other people in the New Testament also encountered the risen Lord, none of them was specifically instructed to write down what they had seen so it could be read by others. What John saw is for all believers everywhere and every time.

John uses physical descriptions to record his vision of Christ, but these descriptions are also deeply symbolic about Jesus' nature. First, Jesus is wearing a flowing robe and a golden band around His chest (see Revelation 1:13), which refers to His role as the great High Priest of His people. His hair is "white like wool" (verse 14), which speaks of His wisdom and eternal nature.

Jesus' eyes are far different than when John saw them last. Gone is the compassion that the disciple likely remembered. In its place are flames capable of penetrating the deepest part of the soul. His feet are like brass, symbolizing His power to judge the nations. His voice is like the roar of many waters, symbolizing its power to be heard across the realm of the earth (see verses 14–15).

Jesus is holding seven stars in his right hand. In John's day, the right hand was a symbol of power and safety, and the seven stars are identified as the seven angels who were sent to guide and protect those congregations. The sword that comes out of Jesus' mouth represents the Word of God, which He will use to judge humanity. The brightness of Christ's face indicates that His light will illuminate a dark and sinful world (see verse 16).

Taken together, these images reveal Jesus as the Holy One who is coming to judge the works of His church. All believers will stand before Him as He evaluates their deeds. We may imagine ourselves reacting as John did at such a prospect—by falling down in a dead faint—but we must remember He is the same Savior in whom we have put our trust. So, while the images may seem alarming, we have nothing to fear. In fact, we can take comfort from this passage.

Jesus not only knows the future but also lives in it just as comfortably as He does in what has been. He holds all power in His hands, yet He invites us to draw near and walk with Him. He sees everything that lies ahead for each one of us and says to us all, "Do not be afraid!"

JOURNALING YOUR RESPONSE

How should Jesus' assurance about the future impact the way you live in the present?

LETTERS TO SEVEN CHURCHES

Revelation 2:1–3:22

GETTING STARTED

What praise and constructive criticism have you heard people offer about your church?

_____

_____

_____

_____

_____

_____

_____

_____

_____

_____

_____

_____

SETTING THE STAGE

The second and third chapters of Revelation contain letters written to seven literal churches located in the Roman province of Asia Minor at the end of the first century AD. These churches were located in the cities of Ephesus,

Smyrna, Pergamos, Thyatira, Sardis, Philadelphia, and Laodicea. Although the entire book was to go to all seven churches (and to believers everywhere), these individual letters were addressed to these specific churches.

Jesus begins each letter with the phrase, "I know your works," and He gives a promise to each person "who overcomes." The letters also follow a consistent format: (1) an instruction is given to John to write down the words, (2) Jesus reveals His knowledge of the deeds—both the good and the bad—of the people in each church, (3) a verdict is rendered based on their acts, and (4) an exhortation is given to heed Jesus' warnings and persevere.

Beyond those similarities, the message of each letter is tailored to the specific needs, issues, and concerns in the church to which it is addressed. For this reason, we must read each in its own context. Even so, one of the remarkable things about these letters is that Jesus' words to the seven first-century churches can be applied to the churches of *every* era—including ours today. These letters can be seen as "tests" for the modern church.

The risen Lord, with "His eyes like a flame of fire" (1:14), is searching the hearts of His people to determine their true character. The results of this probing and searching are as revealing—and as convicting—in our world today as they were some 2,000 years ago. In truth, many problems faced by our modern church could be solved by simply reading the recommendations of our Lord to these churches in Asia.

EXPLORING THE TEXT

Letters to Ephesus and Smyrna (Revelation 2:1–11)

[1] "To the angel of the church of Ephesus write,

'These things says He who holds the seven stars in His right hand, who walks in the midst of the seven golden lampstands: [2] "I know your works, your labor, your patience, and that you cannot bear those who are evil. And you have tested those who say they are apostles and are not, and have found them liars; [3] and you have persevered and have patience, and have labored for My name's sake and have not become weary. ⁴ Nevertheless I have this against you, that you have left your first love. ⁵ Remember therefore from where you have fallen; repent and do the first works, or else I will come to you quickly and remove your lampstand from its place—unless you repent. ⁶ But this you have, that you hate the deeds of the Nicolaitans, which I also hate.

⁷ "He who has an ear, let him hear what the Spirit says to the churches. To him who overcomes I will give to eat from the tree of life, which is in the midst of the Paradise of God." '

⁸ "And to the angel of the church in Smyrna write,

'These things says the First and the Last, who was dead, and came to life: ⁹ "I know your works, tribulation, and poverty (but you are rich); and I know the blasphemy of those who say they are Jews and are not, but are a synagogue of Satan. ¹⁰ Do not fear any of those things which you are about to suffer. Indeed, the devil is about to throw some of you into prison, that you may be tested, and you will have tribulation ten days. Be faithful until death, and I will give you the crown of life.

¹¹ "He who has an ear, let him hear what the Spirit says to the churches. He who overcomes shall not be hurt by the second death." '

---

1. Ephesus was a self-governed city located on the western coast of Asia Minor. It sat at the crossroads of three major highways and was a center for trade. It was also the center for the worship of Artemis, the Greek goddess of fertility. Jesus praised this church for being dynamic, dedicated, determined, disciplined, and discerning. But what was His main charge against them? In what areas did He see room for improvement (see verses 1–6)?

_____

_____

_____

_____

_____

2. Smyrna was a wealthy port city located forty miles north of Ephesus. It was a center of learning in the sciences and medicine—but also a center of emperor worship. By the reign of Domitian (AD 81–95), it had become mandatory for every resident to practice the religion on threat of death. The impoverished members of the church were thus suffering because they refused to engage in emperor worship, and they were also being persecuted by other groups. What counsel does Jesus offer in the midst of their suffering (see verses 9–10)?

_____

_____

_____

_____

_____

_____

_____

_____

_____

_____

_____

Letters to Pergamos and Thyatira (Revelation 2:12–29)

12 "And to the angel of the church in Pergamos write,

'These things says He who has the sharp two-edged sword: 13 "I know your works, and where you dwell, where Satan's throne is. And you hold fast to My name, and did not deny My faith even in the days in which Antipas was My faithful martyr, who was killed among you, where Satan dwells. 14 But I have a few things against you, because you have there those who hold the doctrine of Balaam, who taught Balak to put a stumbling block before the children of Israel, to eat things sacrificed to idols, and to commit sexual immorality. 15 Thus you also have those who hold the doctrine of the Nicolaitans, which thing I hate. [16] Repent, or else I will come to you quickly and will fight against them with the sword of My mouth.

[17] "He who has an ear, let him hear what the Spirit says to the churches. To him who overcomes I will give some of the hidden manna to eat. And I will give him a white stone, and on the stone a new name written which no one knows except him who receives it." '

[18] "And to the angel of the church in Thyatira write,

'These things says the Son of God, who has eyes like a flame of fire, and His feet like fine brass: [19] "I know your works, love, service, faith, and your patience; and as for your works, the last are more than the first. [20] Nevertheless I have a few things against you, because you allow that woman Jezebel, who calls herself a prophetess, to teach and seduce My servants to commit sexual immorality and eat things sacrificed to idols. [21] And I gave her time to repent of her sexual immorality, and she did not repent. [22] Indeed I will cast her into a sickbed, and those who commit adultery with her into great tribulation, unless they repent of their deeds. [23] I will kill her children with death, and all the churches shall know that I am He who searches the minds and hearts. And I will give to each one of you according to your works.

[24] "Now to you I say, and to the rest in Thyatira, as many as do not have this doctrine, who have not known the depths of Satan, as they say, I will put on you no other burden. [25] But hold fast what you have till I come. [26] And he who overcomes, and keeps My works until the end, to him I will give power over the nations—

[27] 'He shall rule them with a rod of iron;
They shall be dashed to pieces like the potter's vessels'—

as I also have received from My Father; [28] and I will give him the morning star.

[29] "He who has an ear, let him hear what the Spirit says to the churches." '

3. Pergamos was located sixty-five miles north of Smyrna and was famous for its sculptures, temples, and library of 200,000 volumes. It was a center for worship of the emperor, Dionysus (god of the royal kings), and Asclepius (god of healing). Many in the church had stayed true to Christ in spite of this hostile environment, but others were following the false teachings of groups known as the "Balaamites" and "Nicolaitans." What warning does Jesus give to these individuals? What does He command them to do (see verses 14–16)?

4. Thyatira was located forty-five miles east of Pergamos. Its residents conducted commerce in wool, linen, dyed goods, leatherwork, tanning, and bronze work. The city was home to several trade guilds, each of which had a patron god and engaged in sexual revelries as a part of their worship. Jesus praised the church for being service-oriented, loving, loyal, faithful, and patient, but He rebuked them for allowing these sexually immoral practices to take root in the church. What was Jesus' message to them in this regard (see verses 20–24)?

Letters to Sardis and Philadelphia (Revelation 3:1–13)

¹ "And to the angel of the church in Sardis write,

'These things says He who has the seven Spirits of God and the seven stars: "I know your works, that you have a name that you are alive, but you are dead. ² Be watchful, and strengthen the things which remain, that are ready to die, for I have not found your works perfect before God. ³ Remember therefore how you have received and heard; hold fast and repent. Therefore if you will not watch, I will come upon you as a thief, and you will not know what hour I will come upon you. ⁴ You have a few names even in Sardis who have not defiled their garments; and they shall walk with Me in white, for they are worthy. ⁵ He who overcomes shall be clothed in white garments, and I will not blot out his name from the Book of Life; but I will confess his name before My Father and before His angels.

⁶ "He who has an ear, let him hear what the Spirit says to the churches." '

⁷ "And to the angel of the church in Philadelphia write,

'These things says He who is holy, He who is true, "He who has the key of David, He who opens and no one shuts, and shuts and no one opens": ⁸ "I know your works. See, I have set before you an open door, and no one can shut it; for you have a little strength, have kept My word, and have not denied My name. ⁹ Indeed I will make those of the synagogue of Satan, who say they are Jews and are not, but lie—indeed I will make them come and worship before your feet, and to know that I have loved you. ¹⁰ Because you have kept My command to persevere, I also will keep you from the hour of trial which shall come upon the whole world, to test those who dwell on the earth. ¹¹ Behold, I am coming quickly! Hold fast what you have, that no one may take your crown. ¹² He who overcomes, I will make him a pillar in the temple of My God, and he shall go out no more. I will write on him the name of My God and the name of the city of My God, the New Jerusalem, which comes down out of heaven from My God. And I will write on him My new name.

¹³ "He who has an ear, let him hear what the Spirit says to the churches." '

5. Sardis was located thirty miles south of Thyatira. The city had once been great militarily and was home to a fortress that had witnessed few defeats in its past. But its residents were now clearly living off the glories of their past, and their "slumber" had caused them to fall into great moral decadence. Jesus called those in the church to "wake up" and engage in a faith that was active and growing. What other directions did He give to them? What did Jesus say would happen if they failed to "keep watch" over their lives (see verses 2–5)?

_____

_____

_____

_____

_____

_____

6. Philadelphia was located twenty-five miles southeast of Sardis. It was a strong fortress city, situated on a major highway, that served as a "gateway" to the Roman territories in the east. Jesus states that even though the church is small and has "little strength," he has set before them "an open door" to proclaim the gospel to the far reaches of the world. What does Jesus say about those who seek to hamper their ministry efforts? What does He promise to those who continue to persevere in following after Him (see verses 9–12)?

_____

_____

_____

_____

_____

_____

Letter to Laodicea (Revelation 3:14–22)

14 "And to the angel of the church of the Laodiceans write,

'These things says the Amen, the Faithful and True Witness, the Beginning of the creation of God: 15 "I know your works, that you are neither cold nor hot. I could wish you were cold or hot. 16 So then, because you are lukewarm, and neither cold nor hot, I will vomit you out of My mouth.17 Because you say, 'I am rich, have become wealthy, and have need of nothing'—and do not know that you are wretched, miserable, poor, blind, and naked— 18 I counsel you to buy from Me gold refined in the fire, that you may be rich; and white garments, that you may be clothed, that the shame of your nakedness may not be revealed; and anoint your eyes with eye salve, that you may see. 19 As many as I love, I rebuke and chasten. Therefore be zealous and repent. 20 Behold, I stand at the door and knock. If anyone hears My voice and opens the door, I will come in to him and dine with him, and he with Me. 21 To him who overcomes I will grant to sit with Me on My throne, as I also overcame and sat down with My Father on His throne.

22 "He who has an ear, let him hear what the Spirit says to the churches." ' "

---

7. Laodicea was located forty-five miles southeast of Philadelphia and 100 miles east of Ephesus. The residents received their water from hot springs located six miles to the south that cooled to lukewarm as the water travelled along an aqueduct into the city. How does Jesus use this imagery to describe the nature of the church's faith (see verses 15–17)?

8. Laodicea was an important center for trade, and its wealthy citizens prided themselves on being self-sufficient. Evidently, this same attitude had infiltrated the church, and the believers had grown ignorant of their dependence on Christ. What does Jesus say to help them recognize their true condition? What is His invitation to them (see verses 17–21).

_____

_____

_____

REVIEWING THE STORY

In this section of Revelation, John relates seven messages from Jesus to seven churches located in the Roman province of Asia Minor. Jesus praises those in Ephesus for their dedication and discipline but rebukes them for losing their first love. He encourages those in Smyrna to remain faithful in the midst of their suffering and persecution—and warns more suffering will come. He praises those in Pergamos for holding fast to their faith and urges them to stay diligent in the midst of pagan influences. He praises those in Thyatira for their love and service but rebukes them for allowing sexual immorality to take root. He rebukes those in Sardis for being spiritually dead and commands them to wake up and be watchful. He commends those in Philadelphia for being faithful and encourages them to persevere. Finally He rebukes those in Laodicea for being lukewarm in their faith and for their attitude of self-sufficiency.

9. What promise is given to those in Ephesus and Smyrna who overcome (see Revelation 2:7, 11)?

_____

_____

_____

10. What promise is given to those in Pergamos and Thyatira who overcome (see Revelation 2:17, 26–27)?

11. What promise is given to those in Sardis and Philadelphia who overcome (see Revelation 3:5, 12)?

12. What promise is given to those in Laodicea who overcome (see Revelation 3:21)?

APPLYING THE MESSAGE

13. Which words of praise from Jesus to the seven churches could apply to your church?

_____

_____

_____

_____

_____

_____

_____

14. Which words of warning or instruction from Jesus could apply to your church?

_____

_____

_____

_____

_____

_____

_____

REFLECTING ON THE MEANING

The letters that Jesus instructs John to write down for the seven churches are profound and provocative. But the question arises as to _how they should be interpreted._ After all, these were specific letters from Jesus to specific churches located in Asia Minor who were each facing their own specific setbacks, challenges, and problems. How do these words from Jesus apply to churches today? Bible scholars have identified three different viewpoints to help answer this question.

First, the *practical viewpoint*. The seven churches in Asia Minor were doing some things right and some things wrong. Jesus commended them for the things they were doing well and rebuked them in the areas they were falling short. By way of example, we can gain practical insights into our own spiritual lives by studying His words to them. Furthermore, we can learn from their example in history. Once a bright spot in Christendom, the region of Asia Minor (modern-day Turkey) is a dark place spiritually. This should serve as a warning to us today.

Second, the *perennial viewpoint*. At any given time, there are churches just like the seven described In Revelation 2–3. There are individual Christians just like them as well—some who have lost their first love (like the Ephesus church) or who are being persecuted (like the Smyrna church). The struggles that plagued the seven churches were anything but first-century problems. The details may vary from time period to time period, but the root issues remain. As a result, at any time in history, churches and individuals can learn from these seven churches.

Third, the *prophetic viewpoint*. The seven churches represent stages of church history. Ephesus represents the era from AD 33–100, when theological error crept into the church. Smyrna represents AD 100–300, when the church faced persecution. Pergamos represents AD 300–500, when Christianity became the state religion of Rome and church and government intermingled. Thyatira represents AD 500–1500, when the politicized version of the "church" in Rome persecuted believers. Sardis represents AD 1500–1700, when the new Protestant Church had difficulty breaking free from Catholicism. Philadelphia represents AD 1700–1900, when the church exploded in revival and missionary expansion. Laodicea represents AD 1900 to the time of the Second Coming of Christ, which encompasses the church of today.

Regardless of which viewpoint we take, it is evident that Jesus' words to the seven churches still have significance to us today. We need understand what they were doing *right* and seek to follow their example. However, we also need to recognize what these churches were doing *wrong*—and heed Jesus' stern warning to alter course while there still is time.

JOURNALING YOUR RESPONSE

Which words of Jesus to these seven churches resonate most powerfully with you?

A GLIMPSE OF HEAVEN

Revelation 4:1–5:14

GETTING STARTED

What images come into your mind when you picture what heaven will be like?

_____

_____

_____

_____

_____

_____

_____

_____

_____

_____

_____

_____

_____

_____

_____

SETTING THE STAGE

When Jesus appeared to John on the island of Patmos, He instructed His beloved disciple to "write the things which you have seen, and the things which are, and the things which will take place after this" (1:19). So far, John has recorded "the things which [are] seen," which represent the vision of the glorified Christ (see 1:1–18). He has also written about "the things which are," which relates to the condition of the seven churches in Asia (see 1:19–3:22).

John will now begin to describe "the things which will take place." This refers to the events that will happen on earth at the end of the "church age," which represents a period of time that extends from Jesus' resurrection to His second coming. As we will discover, the end of this age will usher in a period in which an entity known as the "Antichrist" will be free to do his work—and it will also be a time of God's terrible judgment against the sins of humanity.

It is important to note that up to this point, the Holy Spirit has been present in the churches on earth and among God's people. But as we come to this section in Revelation, we find the Holy Spirit is now up in heaven before the throne of God. As John writes, "Seven lamps of fire were burning before the throne, which are the seven Spirits of God" (see 4:5). This is significant, because in 2 Thessalonians 2:6–8, the apostle Paul writes there is currently a force present on earth who is restraining "the lawless one" from doing his work. This "lawless one," or "man of sin," is the Antichrist, and the Restrainer is none other than the Holy Spirit.

So, when the Holy Spirit—and thus the church in which He dwells—is taken up into heaven, the restraining force will be removed. The Antichrist will be free to do as he pleases, and this will result in a time of tribulation the world has never before witnessed. Truly, as we will begin to see in this lesson, all hell is literally about to break loose on the earth.

EXPLORING THE TEXT

The Throne Room of Heaven (Revelation 4:1–5)

¹ After these things I looked, and behold, a door standing open in heaven. And the first voice which I heard was like a trumpet

speaking with me, saying, "Come up here, and I will show you things which must take place after this."

[2] Immediately I was in the Spirit; and behold, a throne set in heaven, and One sat on the throne. [3] And He who sat there was like a jasper and a sardius stone in appearance; and there was a rainbow around the throne, in appearance like an emerald. [4] Around the throne were twenty-four thrones, and on the thrones I saw twenty-four elders sitting, clothed in white robes; and they had crowns of gold on their heads. [5] And from the throne proceeded lightnings, thunderings, and voices. Seven lamps of fire were burning before the throne, which are the seven Spirits of God.

---

1. The Bible reveals that no one can look on God's face and live (see Exodus 33:20). So, when John looks into heaven, what he sees is only the *appearance* of God—and he tries his best to describe what he is seeing. What imagery does he use to describe the glory of that place? What impact does the presence of God obviously have on John (see verses 1–3)?

_____

_____

_____

_____

2. The presence of the twenty-four elders, who represent the church, indicates that God's people will be with Him in heaven by this point and will not endure the coming Tribulation. God's throne is depicted in the Bible as one of grace for His people (see Hebrews 4:16). But how is it depicted in this passage (see Revelation 4:4–5)?

_____

_____

_____

The Living Creatures (Revelation 4:6–11)

6 Before the throne there was a sea of glass, like crystal. And in the midst of the throne, and around the throne, were four living creatures full of eyes in front and in back. 7 The first living creature was like a lion, the second living creature like a calf, the third living creature had a face like a man, and the fourth living creature was like a flying eagle. 8 The four living creatures, each having six wings, were full of eyes around and within. And they do not rest day or night, saying:

> "Holy, holy, holy,
> Lord God Almighty,
> Who was and is and is to come!"

9 Whenever the living creatures give glory and honor and thanks to Him who sits on the throne, who lives forever and ever, 10 the twenty-four elders fall down before Him who sits on the throne and worship Him who lives forever and ever, and cast their crowns before the throne, saying:

> 11 "You are worthy, O Lord,
> To receive glory and honor and power;
> For You created all things,
> And by Your will they exist and were created."

3. The "four living creatures" that John sees in his vision resemble the beings that Isaiah and Ezekiel observed in their visions (see Isaiah 6:1–3; Ezekiel 1:5–10; 10:9–14). They are "full of eyes" and have knowledge of God and His purposes. Each of their faces (lion, calf, man, eagle) suggest qualities that belong to God (supremacy, power, humility, swiftness of action). These beings lead in delivering God's judgment to earth. But what else are they leading here? What are these angelic beings doing in heaven (see Revelation 4:6–8)?

_____

_____

_____

_____

4. The twenty-four elders (who represent the church) offer their worship to God in response to the glory and honor the four living creatures bestow on God. What is the significance of them casting their crowns before God? For what do they praise Him (see verses 9–11)?

_____

_____

_____

_____

The Lamb Takes the Scroll (Revelation 5:1–7)

¹ And I saw in the right hand of Him who sat on the throne a scroll written inside and on the back, sealed with seven seals. ² Then I saw a strong angel proclaiming with a loud voice, "Who is worthy to open the scroll and to loose its seals?" ³ And no one in heaven or on the earth or under the earth was able to open the scroll, or to look at it.

⁴ So I wept much, because no one was found worthy to open and read the scroll, or to look at it. ⁵ But one of the elders said to me, "Do not weep. Behold, the Lion of the tribe of Judah, the Root of David, has prevailed to open the scroll and to loose its seven seals."

⁶ And I looked, and behold, in the midst of the throne and of the four living creatures, and in the midst of the elders, stood a Lamb as though it had been slain, having seven horns and seven eyes, which are the seven Spirits of God sent out into all the earth.

⁷ Then He came and took the scroll out of the right hand of Him who sat on the throne.

---

5. John sees that the One seated on the throne has a scroll in His hand. There is writing on the front and back, indicating that nothing more can be added to it. There are also seven seals on each portion of the scroll, which represent judgments that will be rendered by God as each seal is broken. However, what is the problem when it comes to opening the scroll? How does John react when he learns of the problem (see verses 1–4)?

_____

_____

_____

_____

_____

6. One of the elders approaches John and tells him not to weep, for there is one in heaven who has the power to break the seals. The elder describes this individual as "the Lion of the tribe of Judah" and "the Root of David" (see Genesis 49:9–10; Isaiah 11:1, 10; Jeremiah 23:5). The scroll is likely the title deed to the earth, and with each broken seal, this man will reclaim a portion of the earth that rightfully belongs to God. How does John describe the appearance of this individual? Why is that significant (see Revelation 5:5–7)?

_____

_____

_____

_____

_____

Worthy Is the Lamb (Revelation 5:8–14)

[8] Now when He had taken the scroll, the four living creatures and the twenty-four elders fell down before the Lamb, each having a harp, and golden bowls full of incense, which are the prayers of the saints. [9] And they sang a new song, saying:

> "You are worthy to take the scroll,
> And to open its seals;
> For You were slain,
> And have redeemed us to God by Your blood
> Out of every tribe and tongue and people and nation,
> [10] And have made us kings and priests to our God;
> And we shall reign on the earth."

[11] Then I looked, and I heard the voice of many angels around the throne, the living creatures, and the elders; and the number of them was ten thousand times ten thousand, and thousands of thousands, [12] saying with a loud voice:

> "Worthy is the Lamb who was slain
> To receive power and riches and wisdom,
> And strength and honor and glory and blessing!"

[13] And every creature which is in heaven and on the earth and under the earth and such as are in the sea, and all that are in them, I heard saying:

> "Blessing and honor and glory and power
> Be to Him who sits on the throne,
> And to the Lamb, forever and ever!"

[14] Then the four living creatures said, "Amen!" And the twenty-four elders fell down and worshiped Him who lives forever and ever.

7. John writes that the four living creatures and the elders change their song once they see the Lamb take the scroll. They each have a harp (a musical instrument used in worship) and bowls filled with incense (the prayers of the saints—which are about to be fulfilled with the arrival of God's kingdom on earth). What do the living creatures and elders proclaim about the Lamb in their song? What do they say that He alone has done (see verses 8–10)?

_____

_____

_____

_____

_____

8. John discovers that there is a multitude of angels—too numerous to count—surrounding the throne of God. This angelic host also proclaims the Lamb is worthy to open the scroll and reclaim control of planet earth. With the opening of the seals, God's purposes are about to be fulfilled. What is the reaction in heaven _and_ on earth (see verses 13–14)?

_____

_____

_____

_____

_____

REVIEWING THE STORY

The scene of John's vision shifts from earth to heaven, where he is given a glimpse of God's throne room. The Lord's throne is surrounded by twenty-four other thrones, each occupied by elders wearing white robes and golden crowns. Lightnings and thunderings issue from the throne, and seven lamps of fire burn in front of it. Four creatures—with the appearance of a lion, a calf, and man, and an eagle—offer nonstop praise to God while the elders fall down to worship Him. John then sees that the One on the throne has a scroll with seven seals, and it is determined that only Jesus—the Lion of Judah and Lamb of God—is worthy to open it. When Christ takes the scroll, first the living creatures and elders, then the angelic host, and then all of creation worship Him and proclaim Him worthy.

9. What does John first hear when the door of heaven is opened (see Revelation 4:1)?

_____

_____

_____

_____

_____

10. What roles do the four living creatures and elders have in heaven (see Revelation 4:9–10)?

_____

_____

_____

_____

_____

11. What words of comfort does one of the elders offer to John (see Revelation 5:5)?

_____

_____

_____

_____

12. What does every creature in heaven and earth proclaim about Christ (see Revelation 5:13)?

APPLYING THE MESSAGE

13. How do you show Jesus that He is worthy of your praise?

14. How can you add more power and meaning to your worship?

REFLECTING ON THE MEANING

In John's vision, the Lamb of God is the only One worthy to take the scroll that commences God's judgment. In taking the scroll, the Lamb *reclaims authority over all the earth.* This is the fulfillment of Daniel 7:13–14, in which One like the Son of Man comes to the Ancient of Days to receive "dominion and glory and a kingdom, that all peoples, nations, and languages should serve Him." Jesus now receives this kingdom from His Father, and during the Tribulation period, He will judge all who are in rebellion against God and establish His rule and reign on earth.

When Jesus takes the scroll, He also receives the worship of heaven. John describes three distinct heavenly groups worshiping the Lamb. The first group comprise the *elders*, who represent the church (see Revelation 5:8). The elders each have a harp and hold bowls that contain the prayers of the saints. Just think about how many of those prayers contain the words, "Your kingdom come. Your will be done on earth as it is in heaven" (Matthew 6:10). These prayers are about to be fulfilled. The elders praise the Lamb for being worthy to open the scroll, for He has redeemed all those who will reign with Him on earth.

The second group who worship the Lamb are the *angels*. As John writes, "I heard the voice of many angels . . . ten thousand times ten thousand, and thousands of thousands" (Revelation 5:11). John is obviously not stating an exact number here but is simply implying that the number of angels present was beyond measure. They shout out the intrinsic qualities of Christ for all to hear—His power, riches, wisdom, strength, honor, glory, and worthiness to be praised (see verse 12). Just imagine the sound of that many angels offering their praise.

The third group who worship the Lamb is comprised of *every living creature* on the earth and in heaven. Every living thing that exists in the animal kingdom—even the birds of the air and fish in the sea—will break forth in praise to the Lamb. John hears this group offering blessing, honor, glory, and power to the One who is worthy to sit on God's throne forever and ever (see verse 13). His words reflect what the prophet Isaiah once wrote about the Day of the Lord: "The wolf also shall dwell with the lamb, the leopard shall lie down with the young goat, the calf and the young lion and the fatling together" (Isaiah 11:6).

When John looked into heaven and saw the throne of God, he became an unwitting observer of *worship in heaven*. It becomes apparent from his description that where the throne of God is, there is worship. Whether the praises are sung by the redeemed or spoken by the angels and the creatures, the central focus of heaven during the Tribulation will be the worship of the Lamb who was slain as He prepares to establish His kingdom on earth.

JOURNALING YOUR RESPONSE

Why do you believe that Jesus is worthy of your worship?

THE SEAL JUDGMENTS

Revelation 6:1–7:17

GETTING STARTED

What course of action do you take when God confronts you with your sin?

_____

_____

_____

_____

_____

_____

_____

_____

_____

_____

_____

_____

_____

_____

SETTING THE STAGE

A cursory look at our world reveals some terrifying realities—wars, starvation, diseases, dictators, biological terrorism . . . the list goes on. Some might think the cataclysmic events that the Bible calls the Tribulation has already begun. But in reality, these are just birth pangs of something far worse to come—and those events begin in this next section of Revelation.

Previously, we saw that John followed Jesus' instructions to write down the things he saw (see Revelation 1), the things which are (see Revelation 2–3), and the things to come, beginning with the scene around God's throne in heaven (see Revelation 4–5). It was there that John witnessed Jesus—the Lion of Judah and Lamb of God—taking the scroll from the One on the throne. John also saw seven seals on the scroll, each representing a coming judgment.

As we will see in this lesson, the breaking of the first four seals releases four horsemen who bring war, famine, and death. In our day, the idea of a horse being an instrument of judgment seems unusual. But in the biblical world, the horse would have been readily understood as such a metaphor. In battle, the strength and fearlessness of the horse were respected (see, for example, Job 39:19–25). In fact, the horse was thought more of as a weapon of war than it was as an agricultural asset or mode of transportation.

Four times in this section of Revelation, we read one of the four living creatures saying, "Come and see" (6:1, 3, 5, 7). In most translations of the Bible, the command is directed to John. However, he is already there, so it might be better to read the word using its alternate meaning: *go* or *proceed*. The command to "come and see" thus issues the command for each of the four horsemen to "go out" and "proceed forth" in fulfilling their mission of executing judgment against the earth.

EXPLORING THE TEXT

The First Four Seal Judgments (Revelation 6:1–8)

> [1] Now I saw when the Lamb opened one of the seals; and I heard one of the four living creatures saying with a voice like thunder, "Come and see." [2] And I looked, and behold, a white horse. He who sat on it had a bow; and a crown was given to him, and he went out conquering and to conquer.

³ When He opened the second seal, I heard the second living creature saying, "Come and see." ⁴ Another horse, fiery red, went out. And it was granted to the one who sat on it to take peace from the earth, and that people should kill one another; and there was given to him a great sword.

⁵ When He opened the third seal, I heard the third living creature say, "Come and see." So I looked, and behold, a black horse, and he who sat on it had a pair of scales in his hand. ⁶ And I heard a voice in the midst of the four living creatures saying, "A quart of wheat for a denarius, and three quarts of barley for a denarius; and do not harm the oil and the wine."

⁷ When He opened the fourth seal, I heard the voice of the fourth living creature saying, "Come and see." ⁸ So I looked, and behold, a pale horse. And the name of him who sat on it was Death, and Hades followed with him. And power was given to them over a fourth of the earth, to kill with sword, with hunger, with death, and by the beasts of the earth.

---

1. The rider of the white horse carries a bow with no arrows and wears a crown that "was given to him." While some scholars believe this rider is Christ, it is more likely that he represents the Antichrist, who has his power given to him and carries no arrows because he conquers in the name of a false peace. The rider of the red horse personifies war—the red color speaking to the shedding of blood. What is each rider's purpose (see verses 1–4)?

2. The rider of the black horse represents famine, which often occurs as a result of war. While the rich will not suffer as much—their "oil and wine" will not be harmed—the average person will border on starvation. The rider of the pale horse represents Death, with Hades following close behind. What power will God give to these riders (see verses 5–8)?

_____

_____

_____

_____

The Fifth and Sixth Seals (Revelation 6:9–17)

[9] When He opened the fifth seal, I saw under the altar the souls of those who had been slain for the word of God and for the testimony which they held. [10] And they cried with a loud voice, saying, "How long, O Lord, holy and true, until You judge and avenge our blood on those who dwell on the earth?" [11] Then a white robe was given to each of them; and it was said to them that they should rest a little while longer, until both the number of their fellow servants and their brethren, who would be killed as they were, was completed.

[12] I looked when He opened the sixth seal, and behold, there was a great earthquake; and the sun became black as sackcloth of hair, and the moon became like blood. [13] And the stars of heaven fell to the earth, as a fig tree drops its late figs when it is shaken by a mighty wind. [14] Then the sky receded as a scroll when it is rolled up, and every mountain and island was moved out of its place. [15] And the kings of the earth, the great men, the rich men, the commanders, the mighty men, every slave and every free man, hid themselves in the caves and in the rocks of the mountains, [16] and said to the mountains and rocks, "Fall on us and hide us from the face of Him who sits on the throne and from the wrath of the Lamb! [17] For the great day of His wrath has come, and who is able to stand?"

3. When the fifth seal is opened, John sees the "souls of those who had been slain for the word of God" under the altar and hears their cries for justice. Given that believers in Christ are raptured at the *beginning* of the Tribulation, these souls represent those who come to faith *during* the Tribulation. Although the passage doesn't describe the events of the fifth seal, what clues does it offer? What is given to these individuals (see verses 9–11)?

_____

_____

_____

_____

4. The breaking of the sixth seal ushers in a series of catastrophic events. Although the natural phenomena that are described—an earthquake, a blockage of sunlight, a meteor shower—are not unusual as *individual* events, the severity of these *collective* events will be unprecedented on earth. How will the people respond to this crisis (see verses 12–17)?

_____

_____

_____

_____

The Sealed of Israel (Revelation 7:1–8)

¹ After these things I saw four angels standing at the four corners of the earth, holding the four winds of the earth, that the wind should not blow on the earth, on the sea, or on any tree. ² Then I saw another angel ascending from the east, having the seal of the living God. And he cried with a loud voice to the four angels to whom it was granted to harm the earth and the sea, ³ saying, "Do not harm the

earth, the sea, or the trees till we have sealed the servants of our God on their foreheads." [4] And I heard the number of those who were sealed. One hundred and forty-four thousand of all the tribes of the children of Israel were sealed:

[5] of the tribe of Judah twelve thousand were sealed;
of the tribe of Reuben twelve thousand were sealed;
of the tribe of Gad twelve thousand were sealed;
[6] of the tribe of Asher twelve thousand were sealed;
of the tribe of Naphtali twelve thousand were sealed;
of the tribe of Manasseh twelve thousand were sealed;
[7] of the tribe of Simeon twelve thousand were sealed;
of the tribe of Levi twelve thousand were sealed;
of the tribe of Issachar twelve thousand were sealed;
[8] of the tribe of Zebulun twelve thousand were sealed;
of the tribe of Joseph twelve thousand were sealed;
of the tribe of Benjamin twelve thousand were sealed.

---

5. After the breaking of the sixth seal, God demonstrates His control over the events taking place by sending His angels to temporarily hold back further judgments. This "pause" in the action reveals there will be periods of God's grace during the Tribulation. What does He allow to happen at this time during the lull between judgments (see verses 1–3)?

_____

_____

_____

_____

6. In the Old Testament, we read of God "sealing" or protecting His people from impending judgment. He protected Noah and his family from the Flood, Rahab and her family from the destruction of Jericho, and 7,000 prophets in Elijah's day from kneeling before Baal. What can we learn about the identity of the 144,000 whom He seals here (see verses 3–8)?

_____

_____

_____

_____

_____

A Multitude from the Great Tribulation (Revelation 7:9–17)

⁹ After these things I looked, and behold, a great multitude which no one could number, of all nations, tribes, peoples, and tongues, standing before the throne and before the Lamb, clothed with white robes, with palm branches in their hands, ¹⁰ and crying out with a loud voice, saying, "Salvation belongs to our God who sits on the throne, and to the Lamb!" ¹¹ All the angels stood around the throne and the elders and the four living creatures, and fell on their faces before the throne and worshiped God, ¹² saying:

"Amen! Blessing and glory and wisdom,
Thanksgiving and honor and power and might,
Be to our God forever and ever.
Amen."

¹³ Then one of the elders answered, saying to me, "Who are these arrayed in white robes, and where did they come from?"

¹⁴ And I said to him, "Sir, you know."

So he said to me, "These are the ones who come out of the great tribulation, and washed their robes and made them white in the blood of the Lamb. ¹⁵ Therefore they are before the throne of God, and serve Him day and night in His temple. And He who sits on the throne will dwell among them. ¹⁶ They shall neither hunger anymore nor thirst anymore; the sun shall not strike them, nor any heat; [17] for the Lamb who is in the midst of the throne will shepherd them and lead them to living fountains of waters. And God will wipe away every tear from their eyes."

---

7. John now sees a multitude of people, comprised of all races and nationalities, standing before the throne of God. They are clothed in white robes (symbolizing salvation and righteousness) and carry palm branches (symbolizing deliverance and celebration). This group likely represents those who are saved during the Tribulation, primarily as a result of the ministry of the 144,000 witnesses just mentioned. What do these individuals declare before the throne? What is the reaction in heaven to their salvation (see verses 9–14)?

_____

_____

_____

_____

_____

8. One of the elders explains to John that the multitude represents those who have "come out of the great tribulation." Rather than being taken *out* of these afflictions, God's plan was to deliver them *through* their trials, which indicates the gospel will continued to be preached after the church is raptured. What relief will these saints find in heaven (see verses 15–17)?

_____

_____

_____

_____

_____

REVIEWING THE STORY

After taking the scroll from the One on the throne, the Lamb begins to open its seals. As each seal is opened, it triggers a new judgment of God on earth. The first four seals unleash four horsemen who bring a false peace, warfare, famine, and death. The opening of the fifth seal is met by the cries of martyrs for their deaths to be avenged. The sixth seal triggers a series of unprecedented natural disasters—a great earthquake, a darkened sun and moon, falling stars, and general terror on earth. Yet the gospel persists, leading to the "sealing" of 144,000 witnesses for Christ who, in turn, reach a countless multitude of people with the gospel.

9. What power is given to Death and Hades during the Tribulation (see Revelation 6:8)?

_____

_____

_____

_____

10. What is the cry of the people on earth when the sixth seal is broken (see Revelation 6:16)?

_____

_____

_____

_____

11. What happens in heaven before the seventh seal is broken (see Revelation 7:2–3)?

_____

_____

_____

_____

12. What did the elder reveal to John about the identity of the multitude (see Revelation 7:14)?

Applying the Message

13. What is your reaction when you read about these judgments that will fall on the earth?

14. What are some ways that God has used you to witness to others about Christ?

Reflecting on the Meaning

In this section of Revelation, the apostle John describes nothing less than hell on earth. As each seal is broken in succession, it unleashes a devastating consequence against the people on this world. By the time the sixth seal is broken, it is as if the judgments from God are shaking the very foundations of the earth—"every mountain and island was moved out of its place" (6:14). When we look at these "sixth seal" judgments, we come up with three inescapable truths.

First, sin brings about horrible consequences. All of human society will be impacted by the breaking of the seals, and no one will be exempt from God's judgment. Even those who profess to not know God will understand that what is happening is coming from the hand of the Almighty Himself (see 6:17). The events of the sixth seal are God's response to the horror of sin. No human being can argue with the Lord when they see His divine displeasure at work.

Second, sin brings about an impulse to hide. Our human instinct is to hide when we are confronted with sin. Adam and Eve were the first to hide from God when they sinned, and we have been doing the same ever since. During the Tribulation, people will hide themselves any way they can—ostensibly to protect themselves from physical harm, but in reality to protect themselves from the all-seeing eye of God. Thankfully, through Jesus Christ, we no longer have to hide from God because the guilt and shame of our sin have been removed.

Third, sin brings about a hardness of heart. Sin can so harden the human heart that people would rather face the terrible consequences of their mistakes than admit their guilt and be forgiven. In his vision, John sees people crying out—praying, in a sense—for mountains to fall on them and shield them from God's presence. You would think these people would feel compelled at this point to fall on their faces and repent. But instead, we find they would rather die. This is the sad result of sin's hardening effect on the heart.

The takeaway for us is not to take lightly God's attitude toward our sin. Even for believers, sin is still sin. Seeing God's response to the sin of the world during the sixth seal judgment should motivate us to confess our own sins before God. When we do, "He is faithful and just to forgive us our sins and to cleanse us from all unrighteousness" (1 John 1:9)!

Journaling Your Response

What motivates you to confess your sin to God?

_____

_____

_____

_____

_____

_____

_____

_____

_____

_____

_____

_____

_____

_____

_____

_____

_____

_____

_____

_____

_____

_____

_____

_____

_____

_____

_____

_____

_____

_____

THE TRUMPET JUDGMENTS

Revelation 8:1–9:21

GETTING STARTED

How do you prepare yourself when you know that you are about to receive bad news?

_____

_____

_____

_____

_____

_____

_____

_____

_____

_____

_____

_____

_____

_____

_____

_____

_____

_____

_____

SETTING THE STAGE

Before we look at the events that will transpire after the breaking of the sixth seal, let's take a moment to review what we have covered up to this point. The church of Jesus Christ has been raptured or taken up into heaven before the beginning of the Tribulation on earth. Most of the Jews and Gentiles who have come to faith in Christ during this time have been martyred. On earth, the seal judgments are taking their toll. Plagues, wars, scarcity of food, natural disasters, and persecution have left the world a desolate place.

Yet the end is still not in sight. More judgments are to come when the seventh seal is broken. When it is opened, seven trumpet judgments will be unleashed. When we reach the seventh trumpet judgment, it will sound forth seven bowls of judgment that will be poured out. In other words, the seventh seal contains within it the rest of the book of Revelation and the plan of God for planet earth. Furthermore, as we get into the seven trumpet judgments, we find Satan's presence in the man of sin, the Antichrist, becoming increasingly more manifest.

However, before any of that happens, there is pause. What is about to be unveiled is so serious that it is preceded by a period of silence in heaven. Up to this point, there has been a cacophony of worship taking place—angels, elders, saints, and living creatures all singing and shouting praise to God. But all this suddenly ceases, and there is absolute quiet in the heavenly realm. It is a foreshadowing of the solemn revelation that is about to be made.

EXPLORING THE TEXT

The Seventh Seal: Prelude to the Seven Trumpets (Revelation 8:1–4)

¹ When He opened the seventh seal, there was silence in heaven for about half an hour. ² And I saw the seven angels who stand before God, and to them were given seven trumpets. ³ Then another angel,

having a golden censer, came and stood at the altar. He was given much incense, that he should offer it with the prayers of all the saints upon the golden altar which was before the throne. ⁴ And the smoke of the incense, with the prayers of the saints, ascended before God from the angel's hand. ⁵ Then the angel took the censer, filled it with fire from the altar, and threw it to the earth. And there were noises, thunderings, lightnings, and an earthquake.

1. John reports that all of heaven waits in silence "for about half an hour" after the seventh seal is opened. This time of waiting is followed by the appearance of seven angels holding seven trumpets. In the Old Testament, trumpets were used to call people to war (see Numbers 10). How might that relate to what is happening here (see Revelation 8:1–2)?

_____

_____

_____

_____

2. Before the trumpet judgments are executed, another angel approaches the altar and offers incense and the prayers of the saints to God. In Scripture, we find that incense and prayers are often connected in this manner because both are precious, pleasant, and drift up to heaven. What happens as a result of the believers' prayers (see verses 3–5)?

_____

_____

_____

_____

The First Four Trumpet Judgments (Revelation 8:6–13)

⁶ So the seven angels who had the seven trumpets prepared themselves to sound. ⁷ The first angel sounded: And hail and fire followed,

mingled with blood, and they were thrown to the earth. And a third of the trees were burned up, and all green grass was burned up.

[8] Then the second angel sounded: And something like a great mountain burning with fire was thrown into the sea, and a third of the sea became blood. [9] And a third of the living creatures in the sea died, and a third of the ships were destroyed.

[10] Then the third angel sounded: And a great star fell from heaven, burning like a torch, and it fell on a third of the rivers and on the springs of water. [11] The name of the star is Wormwood. A third of the waters became wormwood, and many men died from the water, because it was made bitter.

[12] Then the fourth angel sounded: And a third of the sun was struck, a third of the moon, and a third of the stars, so that a third of them were darkened. A third of the day did not shine, and likewise the night.

[13] And I looked, and I heard an angel flying through the midst of heaven, saying with a loud voice, "Woe, woe, woe to the inhabitants of the earth, because of the remaining blasts of the trumpet of the three angels who are about to sound!"

---

3. The first trumpet blast from the angel summons hail and fire "mixed with blood," which is reminiscent of the fourth plague against Egypt before the Exodus (see Exodus 9:23–26). The second trumpet causes something "like a great mountain burning with fire" to be cast into the sea, turning it to blood. This is reminiscent of the first plague against Egypt, when the Nile River was turned to blood (see Exodus 7:20–21). What is the extent of the devastation that the first and second trumpet judgment cause on earth (see Revelation 8:6–9)?

4. The third trumpet sends a burning star from heaven into the world's freshwater supply. (The name "Wormwood" refers to a bitter herb found in the Near East.) This judgment is a counterpart to the previous one aimed at the sea. The fourth trumpet darkens one-third of the galaxy's heavenly bodies, which is reminiscent of the ninth plague of darkness against Egypt (see Exodus 10:21–23). What ominous warning does an angel sound after these apocalyptic events (see Revelation 8:10–13)?

_____

_____

_____

The Fifth Trumpet Judgment (Revelation 9:1–12)

[1] Then the fifth angel sounded: And I saw a star fallen from heaven to the earth. To him was given the key to the bottomless pit. [2] And he opened the bottomless pit, and smoke arose out of the pit like the smoke of a great furnace. So the sun and the air were darkened because of the smoke of the pit. [3] Then out of the smoke locusts came upon the earth. And to them was given power, as the scorpions of the earth have power. [4] They were commanded not to harm the grass of the earth, or any green thing, or any tree, but only those men who do not have the seal of God on their foreheads. [5] And they were not given authority to kill them, but to torment them for five months. Their torment was like the torment of a scorpion when it strikes a man. [6] In those days men will seek death and will not find it; they will desire to die, and death will flee from them.

[7] The shape of the locusts was like horses prepared for battle. On their heads were crowns of something like gold, and their faces were like the faces of men. [8] They had hair like women's hair, and their teeth were like lions' teeth. [9] And they had breastplates like breastplates of iron, and the sound of their wings was like the sound of chariots with many horses running into battle. [10] They had tails like

scorpions, and there were stings in their tails. Their power was to hurt men five months. ¹¹ And they had as king over them the angel of the bottomless pit, whose name in Hebrew is Abaddon, but in Greek he has the name Apollyon.

¹² One woe is past. Behold, still two more woes are coming after these things.

---

5. The first "woe" proclaimed by the angel comes to pass with the sounding of the fifth trumpet. John sees a "star" fall from heaven that appears to have a human personality. While the identity of this entity is not named, it seems evident that it is Satan. What does God give him permission to do? What happens as a result (see verses 1–6)?

_____

_____

_____

_____

6. The releasing of the locusts at the fifth trumpet is reminiscent of the plague of locusts inflicted against the Egyptians before the Exodus (see Exodus 10:3–6). However, here the "locusts" are a figurative term for the demons who are released temporarily from hell. What are the descriptions and characteristics of these evil angels (see Revelation 9:7–11)?

_____

_____

_____

_____

The Sixth Trumpet Judgment (Revelation 9:13–21)

¹³ Then the sixth angel sounded: And I heard a voice from the four horns of the golden altar which is before God, ¹⁴ saying to the sixth angel who had the trumpet, "Release the four angels who are bound

at the great river Euphrates." ¹⁵ So the four angels, who had been prepared for the hour and day and month and year, were released to kill a third of mankind. ¹⁶ Now the number of the army of the horsemen was two hundred million; I heard the number of them. ¹⁷ And thus I saw the horses in the vision: those who sat on them had breastplates of fiery red, hyacinth blue, and sulfur yellow; and the heads of the horses were like the heads of lions; and out of their mouths came fire, smoke, and brimstone. ¹⁸ By these three plagues a third of mankind was killed—by the fire and the smoke and the brimstone which came out of their mouths. ¹⁹ For their power is in their mouth and in their tails; for their tails are like serpents, having heads; and with them they do harm.

²⁰ But the rest of mankind, who were not killed by these plagues, did not repent of the works of their hands, that they should not worship demons, and idols of gold, silver, brass, stone, and wood, which can neither see nor hear nor walk. ²¹ And they did not repent of their murders or their sorceries or their sexual immorality or their thefts.

---

7. The second "woe" comes to pass at the sounding of the sixth trumpet. Notice that the command to issue the judgment comes from the "four horns of the golden altar," which refers back to the scene we saw previously of the martyrs crying out to God for vengeance on those who took their lives (see Revelation 6:9–11). God answers their prayers by releasing four (fallen) angels "who are bound at the great river Euphrates" to do their evil on the earth. How do they accomplish their destruction (see Revelation 9:13–16)?

8. The descriptions of the soldiers and horses—fiery breastplates, horses' heads like lions, smoke and brimstone coming from the horses' mouths—speak volumes about the kind of destruction they will bring. By the time their evil work is done, a third of humanity will be killed. Despite this, what will be the attitude of the people who remain (see verses 17–21)?

_____

_____

_____

_____

REVIEWING THE STORY

When the seventh seal is opened, there is silence in heaven for about half an hour, and then seven angels are given seven trumpets to execute the next set of judgments against the earth. The first four judgments strike the vegetation on earth, the seas, the fresh water, and the heavens, effectively destroying one-third of all creation. These events are devastating, but an angel warns the worst is yet to come. The fifth trumpet blast unleashes a literal hell on earth, led by demonic creatures whose appearance and work almost defy description. The sixth trumpet blast frees four angels of death to embark on their solemn work of destruction. Yet in spite of the judgments, those who are still living on the earth refuse to repent.

9. What are destroyed at the first and second trumpet blast (see Revelation 8:7–9)?

_____

_____

_____

_____

10. What are destroyed at the third and fourth trumpet blast
(see Revelation 8:11–12)?

_____

_____

_____

_____

_____

_____

_____

11. What is unleashed on earth at the fifth trumpet blast
(see Revelation 9:2–3)?

_____

_____

_____

_____

_____

_____

_____

12. What was the result of the destruction at the sixth trumpet blast
(see Revelation 9:18)?

_____

_____

_____

_____

_____

_____

_____

APPLYING THE MESSAGE

13. What does this passage reveal about the way that God views your prayers?

_____

_____

_____

_____

_____

_____

14. What comfort can you take in knowing that Satan can do only what God allows him to do?

_____

_____

_____

_____

_____

_____

REFLECTING ON THE MEANING

In this section of Revelation, we see the downward progression of worship that will take place during the Tribulation (see 9:20–21). After the sixth trumpet judgment, the survivors of earth—instead of repenting and calling out to God for mercy—begin to worship idols made of gold, silver, brass, stone, and wood. Worship always dictates works, and John reveals four kinds of works of the flesh that result when these people choose to worship idols instead of God.

The first work of the flesh is murder. We see the devaluing of human life even in our society today. Despite the best efforts of law enforcement, murder rates continue to rise. In many cases, conflicts that were once settled through arguments escalate to lethal violence. If it is this way today, just imagine what it will be like in the spiritually dark days of the Tribulation.

The second work of the flesh is engagement in occultic practices. The word *sorceries* that John uses in verse 21 is a translation of the Greek word *pharmakon*, from which we get our word *pharmacy*. Its original meaning was related to drug-based occult practices. Astrology, witchcraft, and divination were a gateway to demon possession. Much like today, losing control of one's mind through the use of mind-altering drugs will become a natural spiritual way for the devil to come in and take control over a person's life.

The third work of the flesh is immorality. The word for *sexual immorality* that John uses is the Greek *porneia*, which refers to all types of sexual activities outside the bonds of marriage. Even today, we see institutions promoting the breakdown of God's standards regarding sexual purity. Children are taught to engage in "safe sex." Psychologists and psychiatrists focus more on personal fulfillment than on purity. Just as sex dominated the cultures of ancient Greece and Rome before their falls, so it will characterize the culture of the world before its demise.

The fourth work of the flesh is dishonesty. "Thefts" will characterize the Tribulation culture, not only in terms of people stealing food and other goods from one another, but also in the breakdown of honesty across the board. Without the sanctifying work and restraining influence of the Holy Spirit, the human conscience will cease to work. Truth will become a thing of the past. People will do whatever is right in their own eyes.

Twice in the span of two verses, John tells us the people "did not repent" of their evil ways in spite of the judgment they were facing (see verses 20–21). The human heart isn't changed by punishment alone. Only the *gospel* can lead people to true repentance . . . and it is quite possible that only a few people on earth will turn to God during those final days and be saved. This is why *today* is the day of salvation. So make sure that you have shared the gospel message with the people in your world before the day comes when it may be too late.

Journaling Your Response

What do your works—your daily decisions, actions, and priorities—reveal about your worship?

THE TWO WITNESSES

Revelation 10:1–11:19

GETTING STARTED

Who in your life has been a powerful witness to the love and grace of God? Why?

_____

_____

_____

_____

_____

_____

_____

_____

_____

_____

_____

_____

_____

SETTING THE STAGE

As we arrive at Revelation 10, we encounter a "parenthesis" that occurs between the sixth and seventh trumpet judgments. This parenthesis is similar to the one found in Revelation 8, which occurs between the sixth and seventh seal judgments. These narrative parentheses serve the same purpose that punctuational parentheses serve—they convey necessary information that is not part of the flow of the immediate action. The parenthesis of Revelation 8 was the silence of heaven. The parenthesis that occurs in Revelation 10–11 is a little more complex.

To fully appreciate this interlude, we need to consider what has come before it and what will follow after it. As you will recall, the sixth trumpet blast from the angel unleashed a mighty 200-million-strong army to continue the worldwide destruction that constituted God's judgment on humanity. The army's rampage was one in a series of cascading devastations—a set of natural and supernatural disasters—that left the earth's inhabitants with barely time to catch their breath before the next one plunged them into even more intense suffering.

The pause that follows the sixth trumpet emphasizes the fact there is but one more trumpet left to blow before the horrific events of the Tribulation are over. However, as we will see, this realization brings no immediate relief—for the blast of the seventh trumpet will unleash seven *more* judgments against the earth. In terms of suffering, there is still a long way to go until this intense period of trial and tribulation will draw to a close!

The unleashing of Satan and his demons at the sixth trumpet judgment might cause us to doubt God's sovereignty and grace. But the events in Revelation 10 show that God will still be in charge during the Tribulation. Even more, this "parenthesis" reveals that He deeply cares about humanity and wants all to be aware of the dire consequences of rejecting the gospel.

EXPLORING THE TEXT

The Mighty Angel and the Little Book (Revelation 10:1–7)

[1] I saw still another mighty angel coming down from heaven, clothed with a cloud. And a rainbow was on his head, his face was like the sun, and his feet like pillars of fire. [2] He had a little book open in his hand. And he set his right foot on the sea and his left foot on the land, [3] and cried with a loud voice, as when a lion roars. When he cried out,

seven thunders uttered their voices. [4] Now when the seven thunders uttered their voices, I was about to write; but I heard a voice from heaven saying to me, "Seal up the things which the seven thunders uttered, and do not write them."

[5] The angel whom I saw standing on the sea and on the land raised up his hand to heaven [6] and swore by Him who lives forever and ever, who created heaven and the things that are in it, the earth and the things that are in it, and the sea and the things that are in it, that there should be delay no longer, [7] but in the days of the sounding of the seventh angel, when he is about to sound, the mystery of God would be finished, as He declared to His servants the prophets.

---

1. John now sees a "mighty angel" descend from heaven, not a fallen angel like the four who were unleashed at the sixth trumpet judgment. While there is debate over the identity of this heavenly being, three details in the narrative point to it being Jesus Himself: (1) He is clothed with a cloud, which is always associated with deity; (2) He is crowned with a rainbow, which suggests He comes from God's presence; and (3) He has a shining face and feet of fire, which is how Jesus is described elsewhere in Scripture. What does He carry in His hand? What happens when He cries out in a loud voice (see verses 1–4)?

_____

_____

_____

_____

_____

_____

2. John observes the angel standing "on the sea and on the land," indicating His sovereignty over the world. He has the voice of a roaring lion, which is associated with a ruler. He is holding the now-opened book (the seven-sealed scroll)—which we identified previously as the title deed to planet earth. What does He announce (see verses 5–7)?

_____

_____

_____

_____

_____

_____

John Eats the Little Book (Revelation 10:8–11)

⁸ Then the voice which I heard from heaven spoke to me again and said, "Go, take the little book which is open in the hand of the angel who stands on the sea and on the earth."

⁹ So I went to the angel and said to him, "Give me the little book."

And he said to me, "Take and eat it; and it will make your stomach bitter, but it will be as sweet as honey in your mouth."

¹⁰ Then I took the little book out of the angel's hand and ate it, and it was as sweet as honey in my mouth. But when I had eaten it, my stomach became bitter. ¹¹ And he said to me, "You must prophesy again about many peoples, nations, tongues, and kings."

3. For the first time, John is asked to play a role in the visions that are unfolding around him. What image does the voice from heaven use to emphasize the importance of John assimilating the message that he is now being given (see verses 1–9)?

_____

_____

_____

_____

4. The idea of God's plan being fulfilled was sweet to John's taste, but the judgment it involved was bitter to him. What was he instructed to do with this message? How do we see here that God is merciful and desires none to go through these judgments (see verses 10–11)?

_____

_____

_____

_____

_____

The Two Witnesses (Revelation 11:1–13)

[1] Then I was given a reed like a measuring rod. And the angel stood, saying, "Rise and measure the temple of God, the altar, and those who worship there. [2] But leave out the court which is outside the temple, and do not measure it, for it has been given to the Gentiles. And they will tread the holy city underfoot for forty-two months. [3] And I will give power to my two witnesses, and they will prophesy one thousand two hundred and sixty days, clothed in sackcloth."

[4] These are the two olive trees and the two lampstands standing before the God of the earth. [5] And if anyone wants to harm them, fire proceeds from their mouth and devours their enemies. And if anyone wants to harm them, he must be killed in this manner. [6] These have power to shut heaven, so that no rain falls in the days of their prophecy; and they have power over waters to turn them to blood, and to strike the earth with all plagues, as often as they desire.

[7] When they finish their testimony, the beast that ascends out of the bottomless pit will make war against them, overcome them, and kill them. [8] And their dead bodies will lie in the street of the great city which spiritually is called Sodom and Egypt, where also our Lord was crucified. [9] Then those from the peoples, tribes, tongues, and nations will see their dead bodies three-and-a-half days, and

not allow their dead bodies to be put into graves. ¹⁰ And those who dwell on the earth will rejoice over them, make merry, and send gifts to one another, because these two prophets tormented those who dwell on the earth.

¹¹ Now after the three-and-a-half days the breath of life from God entered them, and they stood on their feet, and great fear fell on those who saw them. ¹² And they heard a loud voice from heaven saying to them, "Come up here." And they ascended to heaven in a cloud, and their enemies saw them. ¹³ In the same hour there was a great earthquake, and a tenth of the city fell. In the earthquake seven thousand people were killed, and the rest were afraid and gave glory to the God of heaven.

---

5. The events in Revelation now focus on Jerusalem, the temple, and the Jews' place in end-time activities. The temple, which was destroyed by the Romans in AD 70, has been rebuilt by the Jews during the Tribulation period. John is instructed to measure its dimensions, which is a precursor to judgment. The two witnesses that then appear are most likely Elijah and Moses, returned to life to call the Jewish people to repentance one last time. What powers will they possess during their three-and-a-half-year ministry (see verses 1–6)?

_____

_____

_____

_____

_____

6. After the ministry of the two witnesses is complete, a beast will appear from "the bottomless pit" (indicating his demonic origin), kill the two witnesses, and leave their bodies on display in the streets of Jerusalem. John notes this "great city" is spiritually called "Sodom and

Egypt," which refers to the people's rebellion against God and the state of their moral degradation. What do the residents of this city do when they see the bodies of the witnesses? What then happens that testifies to God's power (see verses 7–13)?

_____

_____

_____

_____

The Seventh Trumpet (Revelation 11:14–19)

14 The second woe is past. Behold, the third woe is coming quickly.

15 Then the seventh angel sounded: And there were loud voices in heaven, saying, "The kingdoms of this world have become the kingdoms of our Lord and of His Christ, and He shall reign forever and ever!" 16 And the twenty-four elders who sat before God on their thrones fell on their faces and worshiped God, 17 saying:

"We give You thanks, O Lord God Almighty,
The One who is and who was and who is to come,
Because You have taken Your great power and reigned.
18 The nations were angry, and Your wrath has come,
And the time of the dead, that they should be judged,
And that You should reward Your servants the prophets
   and the saints,
And those who fear Your name, small and great,
And should destroy those who destroy the earth."

19 Then the temple of God was opened in heaven, and the ark of His covenant was seen in His temple. And there were lightnings, noises, thunderings, an earthquake, and great hail.

7. John notes the "second woe" (covering the events from Revelation 9:13–11:14) has now concluded and the "third woe" (the seventh trumpet judgment) is about to begin. At this point, it is implied that the "kingdoms of the world" are all under the authority of Satan. However, what does the announcement from heaven indicate is about to change (see 11:14–15)?

_____

_____

_____

_____

_____

8. John again sees the twenty-four elders (who represent the church) before the throne of God. When they hear the announcement, they fall down in worship before the Lord. What is the focus of their praise? What happens in heaven after this (see verses 16–19)?

_____

_____

_____

_____

_____

REVIEWING THE STORY

John witnesses a mighty angel descend to earth. He holds a little book in His hand and announces the work of God is almost complete. John is instructed to take the little book and eat it. When he does, he finds it is sweet like honey to his mouth but makes his stomach bitter. After this, John sees two witnesses on earth embark on a powerful three-and-a-half-year mission to redeem Israel. Eventually, the witnesses are killed by the Beast and his forces, and their bodies are displayed in the streets of Jerusalem for three-and-a-half days. The witnesses are resurrected after this time and ascend into heaven. An earthquake falls on the city, killing 7,000 people, but the remainder give glory to God. Next, John sees an angel sound the seventh trumpet, signaling the beginning of the next set of judgments. The twenty-four elders fall down in worship to God, the temple in heaven is opened, and the ark of the covenant is seen.

9. What are the traits of the mighty angel who carries the little book (see Revelation 10:1)?

_____

_____

_____

_____

_____

_____

10. What instruction is John given after he eats the little book (see Revelation 10:11)?

_____

_____

_____

_____

_____

11. What powers are given to the two witnesses (see Revelation 11:5–6)?

_____

_____

_____

_____

_____

12. What declaration is heard after the seventh trumpet sounds (see Revelation 11:15)?

APPLYING THE MESSAGE

13. How have you found God's Word to be both "sweet" and "bitter" in your life?

14. How has God used you as a witness to reach others with the gospel of Christ?

REFLECTING ON THE MEANING

In this section of Revelation, we saw that when the apostle John began to absorb the message that God was giving to him, at first it tasted sweet in his mouth, but then it did not sit well in his stomach. Remember, the "little book" that John was instructed to eat represents the seven seals of judgment. God's truth is always "sweet," but the reality of His judgment can feel "bitter."

However, even in the midst of these judgments, we find that at times this "bitterness" is temporarily pushed aside and we witness the "sweetness" of God's love, grace, and mercy. We find one such glimpse in Revelation 11:19: "Then the temple of God was opened in heaven, and the ark of His covenant was seen in His temple." At the beginning of Revelation 11, John was given a picture of the temple to be rebuilt in Jerusalem during the Tribulation (see verses 1–2). Now he is offered a vision of the temple in heaven. When that temple is opened, in the midst of the cataclysmic events taking place during the Tribulation, we see the ark of the covenant.

The ark represented several different things to the people of Israel. *First, it represented God's power among His people.* The Israelites had followed the ark as they crossed over the Jordan River and entered into Canaan to claim their inheritance from the Lord (see Joshua 3:11–17). *Second, it represented God's law.* The ark contained the tablets with the Ten Commandments that God gave Moses. *Third, it represented God's sufficiency and provision.* The ark contained a pot of manna, the food from heaven that God had used to sustain the Israelites in the wilderness. *Finally, it represented God's gift of life.* The ark contained the rod of Aaron which budded (see Hebrews 9:4).

The presence of the ark in the heavenly temple reminds us that God promises to be with us even in the most difficult of times. He has even promised to be with those in the midst of the Tribulation who choose to accept salvation through Christ! God's covenant promises are the anchor for the soul of everyone who faces overwhelming circumstances.

JOURNALING YOUR RESPONSE

When have you seen God's presence in the midst of your darkest times in life?

THE UNHOLY TRINITY

Revelation 12:1–13:18

GETTING STARTED

What are some ways that Satan persecutes followers of Christ today?

_____

_____

_____

_____

_____

_____

_____

_____

_____

_____

_____

_____

_____

_____

SETTING THE STAGE

The ancient Chinese general Sun Tzu once advised his warriors that if they wanted to achieve success in battle, they needed to *know their enemy and themselves*. While the art of warfare has changed dramatically over the centuries, the truth of this statement has endured. If you want to achieve success over your enemy, you have to understand the strategies your enemy will try to use against you. The more intelligence you have on what your opponent is likely to do, the more effective your defense will be in protecting yourself from attack.

This applies to both physical *and* spiritual warfare. As believers in Christ, we have been sent by God into hostile territory—the kingdom of darkness—to proclaim the truth of the gospel. If we want to be successful in our mission, we have to understand the tactics that our enemy will employ against us. Fortunately, in this next section of Revelation, we are given a glimpse of just how he operates. The scene that John depicts is the final conflict in heaven. The key players are God and Satan. Below them are their respective angels. And below them are the human combatants who will carry out the conflict that is being waged in heaven on the earth.

What is telling about John's description is that Satan is in *heaven* when these events unfold. John states he is there before God's throne as "the accuser of our brethren" (Revelation 12:10). In the book of Job, we find Satan doing the same thing—*accusing* God's faithful servant of only fearing Him because of the protection that He has provided. This method of attack has been in Satan's arsenal from the beginning. At this very moment, he is waging war against God, against heaven, and against all followers of Christ.

However, as John is about to reveal, Satan's freedom to come before the Lord and make these accusations will come to an end. A final confrontation between Michael and his angels and Satan and his demons is about to take place. And when the dust settles, Satan and his evil followers will once and for all be cast out of heaven to wreak their final havoc on earth.

EXPLORING THE TEXT

The Woman, the Child, and the Dragon (Revelation 12:1–9)

¹ Now a great sign appeared in heaven: a woman clothed with the sun, with the moon under her feet, and on her head a garland of twelve

stars. ² Then being with child, she cried out in labor and in pain to give birth.

³ And another sign appeared in heaven: behold, a great, fiery red dragon having seven heads and ten horns, and seven diadems on his heads. ⁴ His tail drew a third of the stars of heaven and threw them to the earth. And the dragon stood before the woman who was ready to give birth, to devour her Child as soon as it was born. ⁵ She bore a male Child who was to rule all nations with a rod of iron. And her Child was caught up to God and His throne. ⁶ Then the woman fled into the wilderness, where she has a place prepared by God, that they should feed her there one thousand two hundred and sixty days.

⁷ And war broke out in heaven: Michael and his angels fought with the dragon; and the dragon and his angels fought, ⁸ but they did not prevail, nor was a place found for them in heaven any longer. ⁹ So the great dragon was cast out, that serpent of old, called the Devil and Satan, who deceives the whole world; he was cast to the earth, and his angels were cast out with him.

---

1. John opens this section of Revelation by stating that "a great sign" appeared in heaven. His use of the word *sign* indicates the images that he is about to relate—a woman and child—refer to something else. While scholars have debated the identity of this woman and child, the Old Testament prophets often referred to the nation of Israel as a woman in travail. The child would thus refer to Christ, who came from the Jewish nation. What does John say happens to the woman and Child after she gives birth (see verses 1–6)?

_____

_____

_____

_____

_____

2. The second sign—the dragon—represents Satan. The Bible states he rebelled against God (see Isaiah 14:12–15), was cast down from heaven (see Ezekiel 28:17–19), and tried to destroy Jesus when He was born (see Matthew 2:16). The war that now breaks out in heaven is thus a *continuation* of the war that has been going on for ages between God and Satan. What does John say will be the outcome (see Revelation 12:7–9)?

_____

_____

_____

_____

The Voice in Heaven (Revelation 12:10–17)

¹⁰ Then I heard a loud voice saying in heaven, "Now salvation, and strength, and the kingdom of our God, and the power of His Christ have come, for the accuser of our brethren, who accused them before our God day and night, has been cast down. ¹¹ And they overcame him by the blood of the Lamb and by the word of their testimony, and they did not love their lives to the death. ¹² Therefore rejoice, O heavens, and you who dwell in them! Woe to the inhabitants of the earth and the sea! For the devil has come down to you, having great wrath, because he knows that he has a short time."

¹³ Now when the dragon saw that he had been cast to the earth, he persecuted the woman who gave birth to the male Child. ¹⁴ But the woman was given two wings of a great eagle, that she might fly into the wilderness to her place, where she is nourished for a time and times and half a time, from the presence of the serpent. ¹⁵ So the serpent spewed water out of his mouth like a flood after the woman, that he might cause her to be carried away by the flood. ¹⁶ But the earth helped the woman, and the earth opened its mouth and swallowed up the flood which the dragon had spewed out of his mouth. ¹⁷ And the dragon was enraged with the woman, and

he went to make war with the rest of her offspring, who keep the commandments of God and have the testimony of Jesus Christ.

---

3. John does not identify the source of the "loud voice" heard in heaven, but many believe it comes from one of the martyrs around the altar (see Revelation 6:9–10). The voice encourages everyone to rejoice that Satan has been cast down and is no longer able to accuse followers of Christ. But what is the "woe" he pronounces (see Revelation 12:12)?

_____

_____

_____

_____

4. When Satan (the dragon) falls to the earth, he immediately sets out to persecute the Jewish nation (the woman). However, just as God's people were once carried "on eagles' wings" (Exodus 19:4) and delivered from the Egyptians during the Exodus, so God will now give His people the "wings of a great eagle" (Revelation 12:14) to deliver them from their enemy. How does Satan respond when he finds his attacks are unsuccessful (see verses 15–17)?

_____

_____

_____

_____

The Beast from the Sea (Revelation 13:1–10)

¹ Then I stood on the sand of the sea. And I saw a beast rising up out of the sea, having seven heads and ten horns, and on his horns ten crowns, and on his heads a blasphemous name. ² Now the beast

which I saw was like a leopard, his feet were like the feet of a bear, and his mouth like the mouth of a lion. The dragon gave him his power, his throne, and great authority. [3] And I saw one of his heads as if it had been mortally wounded, and his deadly wound was healed. And all the world marveled and followed the beast. [4] So they worshiped the dragon who gave authority to the beast; and they worshiped the beast, saying, "Who is like the beast? Who is able to make war with him?"

[5] And he was given a mouth speaking great things and blasphemies, and he was given authority to continue for forty-two months. [6] Then he opened his mouth in blasphemy against God, to blaspheme His name, His tabernacle, and those who dwell in heaven. [7] It was granted to him to make war with the saints and to overcome them. And authority was given him over every tribe, tongue, and nation. [8] All who dwell on the earth will worship him, whose names have not been written in the Book of Life of the Lamb slain from the foundation of the world.

[9] If anyone has an ear, let him hear. [10] He who leads into captivity shall go into captivity; he who kills with the sword must be killed with the sword. Here is the patience and the faith of the saints.

---

5. John has previously described how the entity known as the "beast" will ascend out of hell, kill the two witnesses (Moses and Elijah), and leave their bodies lying in the streets of Jerusalem (see Revelation 11:7–8). This individual, the Antichrist, will receive great power and authority from Satan to do his evil work on the earth. What does John say will cause the people of the world to fear him, follow him, and even worship him (see Revelation 13:3–4)?

6. The picture that John presents of the Antichrist indicates that he will be a charismatic, clever, cultic, and cruel world leader. However, John's use of the phrase "was given," which appears several times in this passage, suggests the beast will only possess the power that *God* allows him to have. What will he do with this power (see verses 5–8)?

_____

_____

_____

_____

_____

The Beast from the Earth (Revelation 13:11–18)

[11] Then I saw another beast coming up out of the earth, and he had two horns like a lamb and spoke like a dragon. [12] And he exercises all the authority of the first beast in his presence, and causes the earth and those who dwell in it to worship the first beast, whose deadly wound was healed. [13] He performs great signs, so that he even makes fire come down from heaven on the earth in the sight of men. [14] And he deceives those who dwell on the earth by those signs which he was granted to do in the sight of the beast, telling those who dwell on the earth to make an image to the beast who was wounded by the sword and lived. [15] He was granted power to give breath to the image of the beast, that the image of the beast should both speak and cause as many as would not worship the image of the beast to be killed. [16] He causes all, both small and great, rich and poor, free and slave, to receive a mark on their right hand or on their foreheads, [17] and that no one may buy or sell except one who has the mark or the name of the beast, or the number of his name.

[18] Here is wisdom. Let him who has understanding calculate the number of the beast, for it is the number of a man: His number is 666.

7. The beast from the earth, or the false prophet, completes the unholy trinity that also includes Satan and the Antichrist. Just as the Holy Spirit points people toward Christ, the role of the false prophet is to point people toward the Antichrist. He appears meek like a gentle lamb but has the heart of a destroyer. What does he have the power to do? What impact does this have on the people still living on the earth (see verses 11–14)?

_____

_____

_____

_____

8. The false prophet will deceive people into building an image dedicated to the worship of the Antichrist. It is likely this image will be set up in the city of Jerusalem as a counterfeit to the temple of God. In some way, the false prophet will make it seem as if this image can speak and condemn people. How will this play into his next strategy (see verses 15–17)?

_____

_____

_____

_____

REVIEWING THE STORY

John is given a symbolic vision of a woman (Israel) giving birth to a Child (Jesus). A dragon (Satan) appears in heaven, casting a third of the stars (angels) to fall to the earth, and attempts to devour the Child as soon as it is born. But the Child is caught up into heaven, and the woman escapes to the protection of the wilderness. A war erupts in heaven, and the dragon is forever cast out. On earth, he again persecutes the woman, but she is protected by God. Next, a beast (the Antichrist) appears and compels many people to worship him. He is given great power—even appearing to survive a mortal would—and deceives many on the earth. He is aided by a second beast, the false prophet, who creates an image to foster worship of the beast and makes it appear as if the image is alive. He takes control of the world economy and forces everyone to accept a mark on their foreheads or right hand to engage in commerce.

9. What are the physical characteristics of the dragon (see Revelation 12:3–4)?

10. Who leads the charge in heaven against the dragon (see Revelation 12:7–8)?

11. What are the physical characteristics of the beast from the sea (see Revelation 13:1–2)?

12. What are the physical characteristics of the beast from the earth (see Revelation 13:11)?

APPLYING THE MESSAGE

13. How do you protect yourself against Satan's lies and schemes?

14. What opposition to God's work have you encountered in your ministry efforts?

Reflecting on the Meaning

One of the key takeaways of this section in Revelation is that Satan has a personality and is able to successfully influence people to accomplish his desires. Yet the effectiveness of his strategies raises some difficult questions. If Jesus truly "disarmed principalities and powers" on the cross (Colossians 2:15), why does it seem as if Satan is winning? Why does evil appear to have the upper hand in the world ? Why is God waiting until the end of history to destroy him?

Perhaps the best way to understand the seeming disconnect between Satan's ultimate fate and his present freedom is to remember that the cross was, first and foremost, a legal transaction. Jesus appeased God's wrath and satisfied His justice. Satan was disarmed as an accuser of God's people because of the sacrifice of Christ. So, legally, Satan was judged and disarmed. But like any legal transaction, there is a difference between legislation and enforcement. The sentence was passed at Calvary and will be enforced in the future. But the church of Jesus Christ can partially enforce Satan's sentence by standing against him on the legal grounds that we have received through the death and resurrection of Christ.

No law will do any good if it is not enforced. Satan *was* disarmed at the cross, but it is up to the church to *enforce* that sentence. We do this by putting on our spiritual armor each day (see Ephesians 6:13–18), resisting his advances so he will flee (see James 4:7), and encouraging one another in love and building each other up (see 1 Thessalonians 5:11). We remember that it takes spiritual weapons to win spiritual battles (see 2 Corinthians 10:4–5). Most of all, we employ the weapon of *prayer* against the enemy. We pray on earth, and God answers from heaven. Between heaven and earth is where the battle takes place!

The day is coming when "Satan, who deceives the whole world . . . [will be] cast to the earth, and his angels [will be] cast out with him" (Revelation 12:9). In the meantime, we must persevere in prayer and seek to enforce the sentence that was levied against him at the cross. As we do, victory will come in our lives.

JOURNALING YOUR RESPONSE

How can you make your prayers more effective as weapons against Satan?

ANGELIC ANNOUNCEMENTS

Revelation 14:1–20

GETTING STARTED

What is your favorite way to worship God?

_____

_____

_____

_____

_____

_____

_____

_____

_____

_____

_____

SETTING THE STAGE

In the movies, we are used to scenes portrayed with hundreds and even thousands of "extras." Today, filmmakers can even digitally multiply a few hundred people into a cast of thousands. But in the days of ancient

Greek drama, these scenes had to be handled differently. A member of the cast would come to the center of the stage, blow a trumpet, and announce a battle, riot, or other event that involved a great crowd had taken place. The announcement would inform the audience of the story line without the need to have numerous people or props on stage.

We see something similar taking place in this next section of Revelation. Angels come to the "center stage" to announce a series of dramatic events that are about to take place during the Tribulation. Several of the scenes described are complete in and of themselves—and do not necessarily appear in chronological order. But each of the announcements serves to inform the reader of a coming event in prophetic history that will affect the lives of the people of God who are on the earth during the days of the Tribulation.

The opening scene in this chapter sets the tone by depicting a joyous worship celebration featuring Christ standing with 144,000 others on the Mount of Zion. Unlike those who have received the "mark of the beast," these individuals have the mark of the heavenly Father on their foreheads. They represent the members of the Jewish race who were redeemed during the Tribulation and will now receive rewards for their faithfulness to Christ.

The scenes depicted in Revelation can get heavy at times. The amount of pain and suffering that we encounter is extensive. But even in the midst of these judgments, God offers a "break" in the action to give us a message of hope and encouragement. Those who call on the name of the Lord—even in the days of the Tribulation—will be saved and rewarded.

EXPLORING THE TEXT

The Lamb and the 144,000 (Revelation 14:1–5)

> ¹ Then I looked, and behold, a Lamb standing on Mount Zion, and with Him one hundred and forty-four thousand, having His Father's name written on their foreheads. ² And I heard a voice from heaven, like the voice of many waters, and like the voice of loud thunder. And I heard the sound of harpists playing their harps. ³ They sang as it were

a new song before the throne, before the four living creatures, and the elders; and no one could learn that song except the hundred and forty-four thousand who were redeemed from the earth. ⁴ These are the ones who were not defiled with women, for they are virgins. These are the ones who follow the Lamb wherever He goes. These were redeemed from among men, being firstfruits to God and to the Lamb. ⁵ And in their mouth was found no deceit, for they are without fault before the throne of God.

---

1. John states that Jesus is "standing on Mount Zion," which was the earthly place God chose for His presence to dwell in the temple. The 144,000 saints of God—comprised of 12,000 from each of the twelve tribes of Israel (see Revelation 7:4–8)—are thus being rewarded for their faithfulness from the most significant place on earth. The voice that is heard is of a loud angelic chorus. What is unique about the song they sing (see Revelation 14:1–3)?

_____

_____

_____

2. John's statement that the 144,000 are not "defiled" likely refers to their spiritual purity, while his reference to them following "the Lamb where He goes" relates to their obedience to Christ. What else does John say about their nature (see verses 4–5)?

_____

_____

_____

The Proclamations of Three Angels (Revelation 14:6–13)

⁶ Then I saw another angel flying in the midst of heaven, having the everlasting gospel to preach to those who dwell on the earth—to

every nation, tribe, tongue, and people— [7] saying with a loud voice, "Fear God and give glory to Him, for the hour of His judgment has come; and worship Him who made heaven and earth, the sea and springs of water."

[8] And another angel followed, saying, "Babylon is fallen, is fallen, that great city, because she has made all nations drink of the wine of the wrath of her fornication."

[9] Then a third angel followed them, saying with a loud voice, "If anyone worships the beast and his image, and receives his mark on his forehead or on his hand, [10] he himself shall also drink of the wine of the wrath of God, which is poured out full strength into the cup of His indignation. He shall be tormented with fire and brimstone in the presence of the holy angels and in the presence of the Lamb. [11] And the smoke of their torment ascends forever and ever; and they have no rest day or night, who worship the beast and his image, and whoever receives the mark of his name."

[12] Here is the patience of the saints; here are those who keep the commandments of God and the faith of Jesus.

[13] Then I heard a voice from heaven saying to me, "Write: 'Blessed are the dead who die in the Lord from now on.' "

"Yes," says the Spirit, "that they may rest from their labors, and their works follow them."

---

3. God now sends an angel to fly through the heavens and announce the gospel one last time before judgment comes. In this action, we see God still seeking to reclaim those on earth from the clutches of the dragon, beast, and false prophet. What is the angel's message? What warning of coming judgment does the next angel pronounce (see verses 6–8)?

---

4. The third angel spells out two options that are left for the people on earth. They can choose to worship the beast, take his mark, and incur the wrath of God, or they can worship God, receive His seal, and incur the wrath of the beast. What torment is described for those who reject God? What promise is given to those who instead choose to accept God and endure the days of Tribulation on earth (see verses 9–13)?

_____

_____

_____

_____

_____

Reaping the Earth's Harvest (Revelation 14:14–16)

¹⁴ Then I looked, and behold, a white cloud, and on the cloud sat One like the Son of Man, having on His head a golden crown, and in His hand a sharp sickle. ¹⁵ And another angel came out of the temple, crying with a loud voice to Him who sat on the cloud, "Thrust in Your sickle and reap, for the time has come for You to reap, for the harvest of the earth is ripe." ¹⁶ So He who sat on the cloud thrust in His sickle on the earth, and the earth was reaped.

5. John's vision now returns to the theme of God's divine judgment on the earth. How does he describe the individual who now appears on the scene in heaven (see verse 14)?

_____

_____

_____

_____

_____

6. When Jesus was on earth, He told a parable about a farmer who sowed "good seed" in a field to reap a harvest (see Matthew 13:37–43). Jesus said He was the farmer, the good seed was the message of the gospel, and the field was the world. Jesus added that at the time of the harvest, a separation would take place between the righteous and unrighteous. How does that relate to what John now witnesses (see Revelation 14:15–16)?

The Wine Press (Revelation 14:17–20)

¹⁷ Then another angel came out of the temple which is in heaven, he also having a sharp sickle.

¹⁸ And another angel came out from the altar, who had power over fire, and he cried with a loud cry to him who had the sharp sickle, saying, "Thrust in your sharp sickle and gather the clusters of the vine of the earth, for her grapes are fully ripe." ¹⁹ So the angel thrust his sickle into the earth and gathered the vine of the earth, and threw it into the great winepress of the wrath of God. ²⁰ And the winepress was trampled outside the city, and blood came out of the winepress, up to the horses' bridles, for one thousand six hundred furlongs.

7. The next angel that John sees also has a "sharp sickle" to continue reaping a harvest on the earth. However, this time the harvest does not refer to the separation of the righteous and unrighteous but to the harvest of judgment that will occur during the final battle of Armageddon. What instruction is this angel given in this regard (see verses 17–18)?

----

8. John describes the coming destruction in terms of a vineyard keeper collecting a harvest from the "vine of the earth" and throwing it into the "winepress of the wrath of God." What does this imagery indicate about the bloodshed that will happen during the final battle? What imagery does John use to emphasize this point (see verses 19–20)?

_____

_____

_____

_____

REVIEWING THE STORY

John opens this section of Revelation with a description of a great celebration. Jesus, the Lamb of God, is standing on Mount Zion, the location of God's temple on earth. He is surrounded by 144,000 members of the Jewish race who have chosen to believe in Him as the Messiah during the terrible ordeals of the Tribulation. They sing a song of praise to Him that only they can learn. John then sees several angels offering pronouncements to the inhabitants of the earth. The first calls the people to come to God. The second states that "Babylon" will fall. The third warns of the dire consequences of following the beast. The fourth states the time has come for Jesus to use his "sickle" to separate the righteous from the unrighteous. A fifth angel also holds a sickle and is instructed by a sixth angel to begin the process of "reaping" God's divine judgment on those who have chosen not to turn to the salvation offered to them in Christ.

9. Who does John see surrounding Jesus on the Mount of Zion (see Revelation 14:1)?

_____

_____

_____

10. What was John told to write down after hearing the announcements of the first three angels (see Revelation 14:13–14)?

_____

_____

_____

11. What happens when Christ wields His sickle on the earth (see Revelation 14:16)?

_____

_____

_____

12. What action did the angel with the second sickle take (see Revelation 14:19)?

_____

_____

_____

_____

APPLYING THE MESSAGE

13. What steps do you take each day to make sure that you are not compromising with the enemy?

_____

_____

_____

14. How are you participating with Christ in sowing His "good seed" on this earth?

_____

_____

_____

REFLECTING ON THE MEANING

The sheer amount of judgment, tribulation, suffering, and death that we find in the book of Revelation can make it seem as if the people on the earth have no hope. However, even in the midst of the violence and terror, the message of the gospel continues to be preached. In this section of Revelation, God actually sends an angel to circle the earth and make one last appeal for people to follow Him. No one who lives during that time will be able to say He was unfair. All who want to find their way to Him will have the gospel message available to them.

Now, we might find the angel's "gospel message" a bit unusual. He mentions nothing about the shed blood of Christ for the redemption of sin, or God's offer of forgiveness, or the need to repent and put one's faith in Jesus. Instead, the angel's two main exhortations are to "fear God" and "worship Him." The emphasis is on God as the Creator of "heaven and earth, the sea and springs of water" (Revelation 14:7). How can this be considered a gospel message? How can this be considered "good news"?

The answer can be found when you consider the state of the people who are still living on the earth during these final days. As we have discussed, the presence of the Holy Spirit and the church will be removed before the start of the Tribulation. This means the men and women on earth will first need to be called back to a basic knowledge of the *existence* of a God who created the heavens and the earth. It is when they come to an understanding that a loving God exists that they can recognize their need to call Him their Savior and Lord. For some of these people, it will be "good news" indeed to learn that salvation is still available to them.

The term *fear God* means different things to different people. For unbelievers, it means to live in terror of His eternal judgment—to realize that one day they will have to answer for their rejection of His Son. But for believers, it means to maintain an attitude of reverence and awe toward Him—to respond to Him in a way that acknowledges His perfection and power. We choose to willingly "fear God," worshiping Him and giving Him the glory that He is due.

Journaling Your Response

What are some ways that you "fear God" and show Him reverence during a typical day?

_____

_____

_____

_____

_____

_____

_____

_____

_____

_____

_____

_____

_____

_____

_____

_____

_____

_____

_____

_____

_____

_____

_____

_____

_____

_____

_____

THE BOWL JUDGMENTS

Revelation 15:1–16:21

GETTING STARTED

How do you tend to response when you witness injustice in this world?

_____

_____

_____

_____

_____

_____

_____

_____

_____

_____

_____

_____

SETTING THE STAGE

It can be distressing at times to see how slowly the wheels of justice turn. Consider, for example, what often happens when high-profile criminals are indicted. These individuals typically have the financial means to hire powerful attorneys to defend them—and these attorneys can keep their cases from coming to trial for years. When their cases *do* finally come to trial, these high-powered attorneys can then plea-bargain their clients' way out of receiving stiff sentences. Justice seems to suffer at the hands of the justice system!

Fortunately, God's system of justice is different. In this next section of the book of Revelation, we get to see that justice system at work as the Lord takes action against those who have terrorized the people of earth during the Tribulation. God will act swiftly and justly in carrying out His sentence against *all* of these individuals who are found guilty. His actions will come in the form of the last set of seven judgments that will be loosed against the earth.

Remember that the first set of judgments came in the form of the seven seals (see Revelation 6:1–17). These were followed by the seven trumpet judgments (see 8:1–9:21). Now come the seven bowl judgments (see 15:1–16:21). Chronologically speaking, the seal judgments may take years to unfold, while the trumpet judgments could happen more quickly. But the bowl judgments will be the swiftest of all, occurring in rapid-fire succession toward the end of the Tribulation. They represent the last things that happen on earth before the return of Christ.

However, before these dire events occur, the scene switches to heaven. In the midst of a backdrop of unimaginable beauty, God's people praise Him for His works, His ways, His name, His holiness, and His glory. In a sense, they establish God's credentials for the readers of Revelation, reminding them that He alone is worthy to dispense the judgments that follow.

Exploring the Text

Prelude to the Bowl Judgments (Revelation 15:1–8)

---

¹ Then I saw another sign in heaven, great and marvelous: seven angels having the seven last plagues, for in them the wrath of God is complete.

² And I saw something like a sea of glass mingled with fire, and those who have the victory over the beast, over his image and over his mark and over the number of his name, standing on the sea of glass, having harps of God. ³ They sing the song of Moses, the servant of God, and the song of the Lamb, saying:

"Great and marvelous are Your works,
Lord God Almighty!
Just and true are Your ways,
O King of the saints!
⁴ Who shall not fear You, O Lord, and glorify Your name?
For You alone are holy.
For all nations shall come and worship before You,
For Your judgments have been manifested."

⁵ After these things I looked, and behold, the temple of the tabernacle of the testimony in heaven was opened. ⁶ And out of the temple came the seven angels having the seven plagues, clothed in pure bright linen, and having their chests girded with golden bands. ⁷ Then one of the four living creatures gave to the seven angels seven golden bowls full of the wrath of God who lives forever and ever. ⁸ The temple was filled with smoke from the glory of God and from His power, and no one was able to enter the temple till the seven plagues of the seven angels were completed.

---

1. John notes that the seven angels he sees in his vision are about to unleash the "seven last plagues," after which time God's judgment against the earth will be complete (see verse 1). However, before this happens, those who gained victory over the beast during the time of the Tribulation sing a song of praise to God. The reference to this being "the song of Moses" likely refers to the words that Moses wrote just before his death, which deal with retribution and judgment (see Deuteronomy 32:39–43). What do these worshipers say about God in this song (see Revelation 15:1–4)?

_____

_____

_____

_____

_____

2. In Old Testament times, the "tabernacle of the testimony" (also known as the Holy of Holies) was the place where the tablets of the law were kept in the ark of the covenant. Once each year, on the Day of Atonement, the high priest would enter the Holy of Holies to offer a blood sacrifice on the mercy seat, and God's justice against sin would be satisfied for another year. What does John now see coming out of this place in the heavenly temple? What happens after the golden bowls are given to the angels (see Revelation 15:5–8)?

_____

_____

_____

_____

_____

The First, Second, and Third Bowls (Revelation 16:1–7)

¹ Then I heard a loud voice from the temple saying to the seven angels, "Go and pour out the bowls of the wrath of God on the earth."

² So the first went and poured out his bowl upon the earth, and a foul and loathsome sore came upon the men who had the mark of the beast and those who worshiped his image.

³ Then the second angel poured out his bowl on the sea, and it became blood as of a dead man; and every living creature in the sea died.

⁴ Then the third angel poured out his bowl on the rivers and springs of water, and they became blood. ⁵ And I heard the angel of the waters saying:

"You are righteous, O Lord,
The One who is and who was and who is to be,
Because You have judged these things.
⁶ For they have shed the blood of saints and prophets,
And You have given them blood to drink.
For it is their just due."

⁷ And I heard another from the altar saying, "Even so, Lord God Almighty, true and righteous are Your judgments."

---

3. As we have seen, John's vision in Revelation is organized around three sets of symbols: seals, trumpets, and bowls. The world was first ruined by *humans* through the seal judgments. It was then wrecked by *Satan* through the trumpet judgments. It will now be reclaimed by *God* through the bowl judgments. What does John say happens when the wrath of God is poured out in the first and second bowl judgments (see verses 1–3)?

_____

_____

_____

_____

_____

4. The emptying of the second bowl results in the oceans of the world turning to blood, causing the death of every living creature in the sea. The emptying of the third bowl extends that judgment to all fresh water sources. How does the angel say these are fitting judgments for those who have shed the blood of the believers (see verses 4–6)?

The Fourth, Fifth, and Sixth Bowls (Revelation 16:8–16)

[8] Then the fourth angel poured out his bowl on the sun, and power was given to him to scorch men with fire. [9] And men were scorched with great heat, and they blasphemed the name of God who has power over these plagues; and they did not repent and give Him glory.

[10] Then the fifth angel poured out his bowl on the throne of the beast, and his kingdom became full of darkness; and they gnawed their tongues because of the pain. [11] They blasphemed the God of heaven because of their pains and their sores, and did not repent of their deeds.

[12] Then the sixth angel poured out his bowl on the great river Euphrates, and its water was dried up, so that the way of the kings from the east might be prepared. [13] And I saw three unclean spirits like frogs coming out of the mouth of the dragon, out of the mouth of the beast, and out of the mouth of the false prophet. [14] For they are spirits of demons, performing signs, which go out to the kings of the earth and of the whole world, to gather them to the battle of that great day of God Almighty.

[15] "Behold, I am coming as a thief. Blessed is he who watches, and keeps his garments, lest he walk naked and they see his shame."

[16] And they gathered them together to the place called in Hebrew, Armageddon.

5. The pouring out of the fourth bowl results in the heat of the sun becoming unbearable to the people on earth. The pouring out of the fifth bowl causes darkness to fall on the throne of the beast and the place where he has established his kingdom. The darkness that God brings on the beast's activities will cause those who put their hopes in him to gnaw their tongues from the pain. Yet how will the survivors still respond (see verses 8–11)?

_____

_____

_____

_____

6. The pouring out of the sixth bowl causes the Euphrates River to dry up, making it possible for an army of 200 million to amass for the coming Battle of Armageddon. These "kings of the earth" have an "unclean spirit like frogs" within them that emanates from the dragon, beast, and false prophet. However, even as these demonic forces gather their forces at the banks of the Euphrates, what final plea does God make to them (see verses 12–16)?

_____

_____

_____

_____

_____

The Seventh Bowl (Revelation 16:17–21)

[17] Then the seventh angel poured out his bowl into the air, and a loud voice came out of the temple of heaven, from the throne, saying, "It is done!" [18] And there were noises and thunderings and lightnings; and there was a great earthquake, such a mighty and great earthquake

as had not occurred since men were on the earth. ¹⁹ Now the great
city was divided into three parts, and the cities of the nations fell.
And great Babylon was remembered before God, to give her the
cup of the wine of the fierceness of His wrath. ²⁰ Then every island
fled away, and the mountains were not found. ²¹ And great hail from
heaven fell upon men, each hailstone about the weight of a talent.
Men blasphemed God because of the plague of the hail, since that
plague was exceedingly great.

---

7. The pouring out of the seventh bowl leads to God proclaiming, "It
is done!" This statement should remind us of Jesus' words on the cross,
"It is finished!" (John 19:30), which signified the conclusion of God's
judgment on Him. What events will quickly follow that signal the end
of God's judgment on the earth has occurred (see Revelation 16:17–19)?

_____

_____

_____

_____

8. The earthquake that God unleashes during the seventh bowl
judgment is so great that it reaches the strongholds of evil. Even the
city of "Babylon," the great religious-commercial system of this world
nurtured by the Antichrist, comes under the sentence of God's justice.
What final acts will occur? How will the people on earth respond
(see verses 20–21)?

_____

_____

_____

_____

_____

REVIEWING THE STORY

John sees those who were put to death for refusing to worship the beast standing on what appears to be a sea of glass mingled with fire. They sing a song of praise to God for His mighty works and the final judgments that are about to fall. When their song ends, the temple in heaven is opened, seven angels step out, and the glory of the Lord fills the place. The angels are then instructed to begin to pour out the bowls. The pouring of the first leads to a scourge of four sores. The second and third bring a plague of blood on all waters on the earth. The fourth results in scorching heat from the sun. The fifth brings darkness on the beast's throne. The sixth dries up the Euphrates River. The seventh and final judgement brings about an earthquake that is so great it impacts the entire world as hailstones also fall from the sky.

9. What does John see when the heavenly temple is opened (see Revelation 15:6–8)?

10. What does the angel proclaim after pouring out the third bowl (see Revelation 16:5–6)?

11. What does God declare after the pouring of the sixth bowl (see Revelation 16:15)?

_____

_____

_____

_____

12. What does God "remember" when the seventh bowl is poured (see Revelation 16:19)?

_____

_____

_____

_____

APPLYING THE MESSAGE

13. What is something about God's nature that you feel is worthy of your praise?

_____

_____

_____

_____

14. How do you respond to the fact that the Lord is a God of mercy _and_ of justice?

_____

_____

_____

_____

REFLECTING ON THE MEANING

The judgment that God directs toward the earth, while sobering in its implications, is no less just than the judgment God directed toward His Son to deal with our sins. If we can understand how God can be *just* and at the same time the *justifier* of sinners, we can understand how His holiness demands that He judge the sins of those on earth who have rebelled against Him. The vision that John sees of the angels coming out from the Holy of Holies in the temple is a perfect way to illustrate this idea that judgment flows from the holiness of God.

Several times in this section of Revelation, we are told that when the bowl judgments fall, the people on earth will still refuse to repent and seek God's mercy (see Revelation 15:9, 11, 21). The takeaway is that those who refuse to drink the cup of God's *salvation* will instead find that they must drink from the cup of His *wrath*. There is no middle ground with God. From the beginning, the choice has been to either accept God's plan or experience God's justice.

Now, it is important to remember that if you are a Christian, these events in Revelation have no direct application to you. You will not be on earth during the seven bowl judgments. However, as with all Scripture, there is an application to be made. If the Lord Jesus Christ came back today, the judgments described in these chapters would take place no later than *seven years from now*. Who do you know who doesn't yet know Christ? If the Rapture occurred today, who would be left behind to endure the seven bowl judgments?

The application of these passages in Revelation should motivate you to use every moment that you have to introduce others to Christ. Resist the temptation to read John's words in Revelation as mere fantasy or fiction. Instead, read them as future fact—and take these seven bowls of God's judgment seriously. Make it your goal today to ask God to give you opportunities to let people know about His Son, Jesus, about His offer of salvation, about His grace and mercy . . . and also about the judgment that is soon to come.

Journaling Your Response

How do you balance God's judgment in this passage with what the Bible says about His mercy?

_____

_____

_____

_____

_____

_____

_____

_____

_____

_____

_____

_____

_____

_____

_____

_____

_____

_____

_____

_____

_____

_____

_____

_____

_____

_____

_____

_____

_____

_____

BABYLON FALLS

Revelation 17:1–18:24

GETTING STARTED

What do you know about Babylon based on your reading of the Bible?

_____

_____

_____

_____

_____

_____

_____

_____

_____

_____

_____

_____

_____

_____

SETTING THE STAGE

Before beginning an in-depth study of Revelation 17–18, it will be helpful
to remember that these two chapters are parenthetical in the overall flow

of the chronology of the book. The end of Revelation 16 described the seventh bowl judgment (verses 17–21), the details of which are continued in Revelation 19. The information provided in Revelation 17–18 thus serve to present information that can help us better understand the final events of the Great Tribulation.

We read of one of these events at the beginning of Revelation 17, where John paints a startling picture of a worldwide religious system that will arise during the end times. This system is depicted in John's vision as a "woman . . . arrayed in purple and scarlet," with the name "BABYLON THE GREAT" written on her forehead (verses 4–5). The woman is sitting on a scarlet beast, revealing the close relationship between her and the Antichrist. In fact, we find that this religious system will be sanctioned by the Antichrist . . . before he ultimately turns on it and destroys it during the final days of the Great Tribulation.

In Revelation 18, John continues the theme of "Babylon" that he began in chapter 17. However, instead of describing its religious ramifications, he tells of the economic and commercial aspects of this world system. He reveals that Babylon the third city out of which the Antichrist will operate during the Tribulation: Rome will be the political base, Jerusalem the religious base, and Babylon the commercial and financial base. However, not even this system will stand, and it will be destroyed in the days before the second coming of Christ.

It is interesting to note that Babylon is the most frequently mentioned city in the Bible besides Jerusalem, occurring more than 250 times. The city is always presented as a place that functions in opposition to God. In fact, the original purpose of the Tower of Babel in Genesis, from which the city derived its name, was for humans to prove their independence from the controlling influence of God. Later on, when King Nebuchadnezzar restored the city to prominence in the world, he declared, "Is not this great Babylon that I have built for a royal dwelling by my mighty power and for the honor of my majesty?" (Daniel 4:30).

That spirit, while not called "Babylon" in our modern world, is still very much alive and present. Today, we would call it *humanism*—a life where humans are the center of the universe. This same spirit of Babylon will be pervasive throughout the earth during the Great Tribulation. But by the end, both the city *and* the spirit of Babylon will be destroyed.

EXPLORING THE TEXT

The Scarlet Woman and Scarlet Beast (Revelation 17:1–7)

¹ Then one of the seven angels who had the seven bowls came and talked with me, saying to me, "Come, I will show you the judgment of the great harlot who sits on many waters, ²ʹwith whom the kings of the earth committed fornication, and the inhabitants of the earth were made drunk with the wine of her fornication."

³ So he carried me away in the Spirit into the wilderness. And I saw a woman sitting on a scarlet beast which was full of names of blasphemy, having seven heads and ten horns. ⁴ The woman was arrayed in purple and scarlet, and adorned with gold and precious stones and pearls, having in her hand a golden cup full of abominations and the filthiness of her fornication. ⁵ And on her forehead a name was written:

MYSTERY, BABYLON THE GREAT,
THE MOTHER OF HARLOTS
AND OF THE ABOMINATIONS
OF THE EARTH.

⁶ I saw the woman, drunk with the blood of the saints and with the blood of the martyrs of Jesus. And when I saw her, I marveled with great amazement.

⁷ But the angel said to me, "Why did you marvel? I will tell you the mystery of the woman and of the beast that carries her, which has the seven heads and the ten horns.

1. John notes the next part of his vision is revealed by "one of the seven angels who had the seven bowls," which indicates this is a continuation of the final bowl judgment. The angel tells John that he will see the judgment of the "great harlot who sits on many waters" and then carries John away into the wilderness. What two figures does John encounter when he arrives there? What descriptions does he provide about them (see verses 1–4)?

_____

_____

_____

_____

_____

2. The woman's clothing and adornment reveal her unlimited prosperity, while her cup filled with "abominations and . . . filthiness" reveal her unholy passions. Her name—"MYSTERY, BABYLON THE GREAT"—calls to mind the pagan roots of her idolatrous religious practices. What does John say this woman has done to God's followers (see verses 6–7)?

_____

_____

_____

_____

The Meaning of the Woman and the Beast (Revelation 17:8–18)

[8] The beast that you saw was, and is not, and will ascend out of the bottomless pit and go to perdition. And those who dwell on the earth will marvel, whose names are not written in the Book of Life from the foundation of the world, when they see the beast that was, and is not, and yet is. [9] "Here is the mind which has wisdom: The seven

heads are seven mountains on which the woman sits. ¹⁰ There are also seven kings. Five have fallen, one is, and the other has not yet come. And when he comes, he must continue a short time. ¹¹ The beast that was, and is not, is himself also the eighth, and is of the seven, and is going to perdition.

¹² "The ten horns which you saw are ten kings who have received no kingdom as yet, but they receive authority for one hour as kings with the beast. ¹³ These are of one mind, and they will give their power and authority to the beast. ¹⁴ These will make war with the Lamb, and the Lamb will overcome them, for He is Lord of lords and King of kings; and those who are with Him are called, chosen, and faithful."

¹⁵ Then he said to me, "The waters which you saw, where the harlot sits, are peoples, multitudes, nations, and tongues. ¹⁶ And the ten horns which you saw on the beast, these will hate the harlot, make her desolate and naked, eat her flesh and burn her with fire. ¹⁷ For God has put it into their hearts to fulfill His purpose, to be of one mind, and to give their kingdom to the beast, until the words of God are fulfilled. ¹⁸ And the woman whom you saw is that great city which reigns over the kings of the earth."

---

3. The angel now explains the meaning of the vision to John. The beast is the one who was killed but came back to life (see Revelation 13:3), which identifies him as the Antichrist. The woman is seated on "seven mountains," which identifies her as Rome, the city built on seven hills. In particular, the woman represents the great *religious–political* power of Rome. What does this imply about the relationship between the woman and the beast (see verses 8–11)?

_____

_____

_____

_____

4. The "ten horns" represent the ten heads of state (or nations) the Antichrist and false prophet will use to administer their power and influence. These horns represent the future government of "Rome" that will one day be established on the earth. This coalition will wage war against Christ but be defeated. What will happen after they have used the woman (the false religious system) to accomplish their purposes (see verses 12–18)?

_____

_____

_____

_____

_____

_____

_____

_____

_____

_____

The Fall of Babylon the Great (Revelation 18:1–10)

¹ After these things I saw another angel coming down from heaven, having great authority, and the earth was illuminated with his glory. ² And he cried mightily with a loud voice, saying, "Babylon the great is fallen, is fallen, and has become a dwelling place of demons, a prison for every foul spirit, and a cage for every unclean and hated bird! ³ For all the nations have drunk of the wine of the wrath of her fornication, the kings of the earth have committed fornication with her, and the merchants of the earth have become rich through the abundance of her luxury."

⁴ And I heard another voice from heaven saying, "Come out of her, my people, lest you share in her sins, and lest you receive of her plagues. ⁵ For her sins have reached to heaven, and God has

remembered her iniquities. ⁶ Render to her just as she rendered to you, and repay her double according to her works; in the cup which she has mixed, mix double for her. ⁷ In the measure that she glorified herself and lived luxuriously, in the same measure give her torment and sorrow; for she says in her heart, 'I sit as queen, and am no widow, and will not see sorrow.' ⁸ Therefore her plagues will come in one day—death and mourning and famine. And she will be utterly burned with fire, for strong is the Lord God who judges her.

⁹ "The kings of the earth who committed fornication and lived luxuriously with her will weep and lament for her, when they see the smoke of her burning, ¹⁰ standing at a distance for fear of her torment, saying, 'Alas, alas, that great city Babylon, that mighty city! For in one hour your judgment has come.' "

---

5. John sees another angel descend from heaven whose splendor is so radiant that it illuminates the entire earth. This angel follows up on the judgment against Babylon's *religious* system (seen in the previous chapter of Revelation) by now proclaiming the fall of its *commercial* system. The announcement is accompanied with a warning to God's people. What does the voice from heaven instruct them to do (see verses 1–5)?

6. The word John uses for *fallen* in this passage means to fall instantly. In other words, the destruction of Babylon will not take place over a long period of time but will happen in a moment—in one single day. By what standard will Babylon be judged? How will "the kings of the earth" who profited from her react to the destruction (see verses 6–10)?

_____

_____

_____

_____

_____

_____

_____

_____

The World Mourns Babylon's Fall (Revelation 18:11–24)

[11] "And the merchants of the earth will weep and mourn over her, for no one buys their merchandise anymore: [12] merchandise of gold and silver, precious stones and pearls, fine linen and purple, silk and scarlet, every kind of citron wood, every kind of object of ivory, every kind of object of most precious wood, bronze, iron, and marble; [13] and cinnamon and incense, fragrant oil and frankincense, wine and oil, fine flour and wheat, cattle and sheep, horses and chariots, and bodies and souls of men. [14] The fruit that your soul longed for has gone from you, and all the things which are rich and splendid have gone from you, and you shall find them no more at all. [15] The merchants of these things, who became rich by her, will stand at a distance for fear of her torment, weeping and wailing, [16] and saying, 'Alas, alas, that great city that was clothed in fine linen, purple, and scarlet, and adorned with gold and precious stones and pearls! [17] For in one hour such great riches came to nothing.' Every shipmaster, all who travel by ship, sailors, and as many as trade on the sea, stood at

a distance ¹⁸ and cried out when they saw the smoke of her burning, saying, 'What is like this great city?'

¹⁹ "They threw dust on their heads and cried out, weeping and wailing, and saying, 'Alas, alas, that great city, in which all who had ships on the sea became rich by her wealth! For in one hour she is made desolate.'

²⁰ "Rejoice over her, O heaven, and you holy apostles and prophets, for God has avenged you on her!"

²¹ Then a mighty angel took up a stone like a great millstone and threw it into the sea, saying, "Thus with violence the great city Babylon shall be thrown down, and shall not be found anymore. ²² The sound of harpists, musicians, flutists, and trumpeters shall not be heard in you anymore. No craftsman of any craft shall be found in you anymore, and the sound of a millstone shall not be heard in you anymore. ²³ The light of a lamp shall not shine in you anymore, and the voice of bridegroom and bride shall not be heard in you anymore. For your merchants were the great men of the earth, for by your sorcery all the nations were deceived. ²⁴ And in her was found the blood of prophets and saints, and of all who were slain on the earth."

---

7. It will not only be the rulers of the earth who will mourn the destruction of Babylon. The merchants and mariners will weep as well, because they will have lost the source of their wealth—their trade in gold, silver, gems, linens, spices, and other luxuries. What will they say about how swiftly God brought about His judgment (see verses 11–19)?

8. The reaction in heaven to Babylon's fall is different from the reaction on earth. The people of God will rejoice and celebrate, for they will see that God has judged the city for its persecution of the saints. According to the mighty angel who takes "a stone like a great millstone" and throws it into the sea, why is Babylon's fate justified (see verses 20–24)?

_____

_____

_____

_____

_____

_____

_____

_____

_____

REVIEWING THE STORY

An angel approaches John, carries him into the wilderness, and shows him a vision of a woman riding on the back of a scarlet beast. The woman is clothed in purple and scarlet, adorned with precious jewels, and holds a golden cup filled with the abominations of her fornications. She is drunk with the blood of the saints and martyrs. The angel explains the beast represents the Antichrist and the woman represents "Babylon" or "Rome"—the counterfeit economic and religious system the Antichrist will use to influence the world. The beast has ten horns, which represent ten "kings" or nations who will unite together to wage war against Christ. After they are defeated, and the Antichrist has achieved his purposes, he will abandon the woman, and it will be destroyed. All those who profited from Babylon's wickedness will mourn their loss, while the saints in heaven will rejoice that they have been avenged.

9. What did John see written on the woman's forehead (see Revelation 17:5)?

_____

_____

_____

_____

_____

10. What will the beast do that will cause people to marvel (see Revelation 17:8)?

_____

_____

_____

_____

_____

11. What does the voice from heaven say about Babylon's sins (see Revelation 18:5)?

_____

_____

_____

_____

_____

12. What did the mighty angel do to illustrate Babylon's great fall (see Revelation 18:21)?

_____

_____

_____

_____

APPLYING THE MESSAGE

13. What are some counterfeit religious systems that you see at work in the world today?

_____

_____

_____

_____

_____

_____

_____

_____

14. What are some areas of compromise with the enemy that God is calling you to flee?

_____

_____

_____

_____

_____

_____

_____

REFLECTING ON THE MEANING

On earth, three classes of people mourn the destruction of Babylon: monarchs, merchants, and mariners. The monarchs mourn because the system in which they have placed their hopes has come to an end. The merchants mourn because the economic hub of the world has spun off its axle and ground to a halt—taking their wealth and prosperity with it. The mariners, viewing the destruction from a distance, mourn because the fall of Babylon signals their own doom.

However, in heaven, three other classes of people rejoice over its destruction: saints, apostles, and prophets. Unrestrained jubilation breaks forth as they recognize God has meted out retribution on the city that had persecuted and martyred them. A mighty angel hurls a great stone, like a millstone, into the sea as a symbol of the city's violent destruction. It is as if the warning that Jesus gave to His followers—"whoever causes one of these little ones who believe in Me to sin, it would be better for him if a millstone were hung around his neck, and he were drowned in the depth of the sea" (Matthew 18:6)—has been carried out against Babylon.

So, how should *we* respond when we read of the judgment and fall of Babylon? The voice John hears from heaven states it plainly: "Come out of her, my people, lest you share in her sins, and lest you receive of her plagues" (Revelation 18:4). The command for God's people to "come out" and be separate from the world is frequently found in Scripture. One of the best-known examples of these exhortations is given by the apostle Paul to the Corinthians, where he tells them not to be unequally yoked with unbelievers (see 2 Corinthians 6:14–18).

In the end, we find there are two key reasons for fleeing Babylon. *First, we need to flee so we are separate from the sins of Babylon.* Judgment is coming on the world system of Satan, and if we are separate from Babylon's sins, that judgment will not fall on us. *Second, we need to flee so we can escape the judgments coming on the Antichrist and those who follow him.* As God has said, these judgments will come swiftly—"her plagues will come in one day" (Revelation 18:8)—so we need to make sure we are nowhere near "Babylon" when these plagues fall.

We cannot think that because the *literal* Babylon lies in ruins today that the *spirit* of Babylon is not alive and well. Staying separate from that worldly spirit is the key to safety in the days ahead. As James wrote, "Friendship with the world is enmity with God . . . whoever therefore wants to be a friend of the world makes himself an enemy of God" (4:4).

JOURNALING YOUR RESPONSE

How do you seek to keep your relationship with Christ free from harmful outside influences?

SATAN IS DEFEATED

Revelation 19:1–20:15

GETTING STARTED

How do you picture the second coming of Christ?

_____

_____

_____

_____

_____

_____

_____

_____

_____

_____

_____

_____

_____

SETTING THE STAGE

Up to this point in Revelation, we have witnessed the earth being ruined by humans and ruled by Satan in the days of the Tribulation. But everything is about to change, beginning in this next section of John's vision. The destruction of Babylon, the capital of the Antichrist's world empire, marks the end of the Great Tribulation. The horrors that have filled the earth through the judgments God has poured out, and through the demonically orchestrated actions of the east, have now been stilled. Darkness is about to give way to light.

The most anticipated event in history is about to take place—the Second Coming of Christ. This episode is emphasized in seventeen books of the Old Testament and in seventy percent of the New Testament. Jesus promised that He would return (see John 14:2–3), as did the angels who spoke to the apostles at His ascension (see Acts 1:11). Yet this abundance of evidence does not keep scoffers from asking, "Where is the promise of His coming?" (2 Peter 3:4). This question is now answered in this portion of Revelation.

The Bible tells us we are not to know the date of Jesus' return, only that it *will* happen. The only "when" we do know is that it will occur seven years after the Rapture of the church. The Rapture starts the end-time prophetic clock ticking, but given that we do not know the date of that event, we do not know the dates of the events that are dependent on it. But one point the Bible makes absolutely clear is that the Second Coming will be a glorious event all the world will witness—both believers and unbelievers alike.

Jesus said His coming would be like the lightning that begins in the east and shines to the west (see Matthew 24:27). His return will illuminate the dark days at the end of the Tribulation like lightning illuminates the pitch-black darkness of a violent thunderstorm. He will be seen riding on a white horse in the midst of that lightning, accompanied by all the saints.

EXPLORING THE TEXT

Heaven Exalts Over Babylon (Revelation 19:1–10)

[1] After these things I heard a loud voice of a great multitude in heaven, saying, "Alleluia! Salvation and glory and honor and power belong to the Lord our God! [2] For true and righteous are His judgments, because He has judged the great harlot who corrupted the earth with

her fornication; and He has avenged on her the blood of His servants shed by her." ³ Again they said, "Alleluia! Her smoke rises up forever and ever!" ⁴ And the twenty-four elders and the four living creatures fell down and worshiped God who sat on the throne, saying, "Amen! Alleluia!" ⁵ Then a voice came from the throne, saying, "Praise our God, all you His servants and those who fear Him, both small and great!"

⁶ And I heard, as it were, the voice of a great multitude, as the sound of many waters and as the sound of mighty thunderings, saying, "Alleluia! For the Lord God Omnipotent reigns! ⁷ Let us be glad and rejoice and give Him glory, for the marriage of the Lamb has come, and His wife has made herself ready." ⁸ And to her it was granted to be arrayed in fine linen, clean and bright, for the fine linen is the righteous acts of the saints.

⁹ Then he said to me, "Write: 'Blessed are those who are called to the marriage supper of the Lamb!' " And he said to me, "These are the true sayings of God." ¹⁰ And I fell at his feet to worship him. But he said to me, "See that you do not do that! I am your fellow servant, and of your brethren who have the testimony of Jesus. Worship God! For the testimony of Jesus is the spirit of prophecy."

---

1. The scene now shifts to heaven in the aftermath of God's judgment on Babylon. In contrast to the mourning we have seen from the monarchs, merchants, and mariners on earth, the hosts of heaven rejoice and praise God when they witness the destruction of the city. What does this heavenly host proclaim about His judgments (see verses 1–5)?

2. The cycle of praise ends with the reverberating sounds of another great multitude who proclaim, "the Lord God Omnipotent reigns" (verse 6). This cry serves as both a conclusion that God has acted sovereignly in His judgments against sin and also an introduction that He will act sovereignly in saving a multitude who will be united forever with His Son. What event is about to take place? What is John instructed to write (see verses 7–10)?

_____

_____

_____

_____

_____

Christ on a White Horse (Revelation 19:11–21)

¹¹ Now I saw heaven opened, and behold, a white horse. And He who sat on him was called Faithful and True, and in righteousness He judges and makes war. ¹² His eyes were like a flame of fire, and on His head were many crowns. He had a name written that no one knew except Himself. ¹³ He was clothed with a robe dipped in blood, and His name is called The Word of God. ¹⁴ And the armies in heaven, clothed in fine linen, white and clean, followed Him on white horses. ¹⁵ Now out of His mouth goes a sharp sword, that with it He should strike the nations. And He Himself will rule them with a rod of iron. He Himself treads the winepress of the fierceness and wrath of Almighty God. ¹⁶ And He has on His robe and on His thigh a name written:

KING OF KINGS AND
LORD OF LORDS.

¹⁷ Then I saw an angel standing in the sun; and he cried with a loud voice, saying to all the birds that fly in the midst of heaven, "Come

and gather together for the supper of the great God, [18] that you may eat the flesh of kings, the flesh of captains, the flesh of mighty men, the flesh of horses and of those who sit on them, and the flesh of all people, free and slave, both small and great."

[19] And I saw the beast, the kings of the earth, and their armies, gathered together to make war against Him who sat on the horse and against His army. [20] Then the beast was captured, and with him the false prophet who worked signs in his presence, by which he deceived those who received the mark of the beast and those who worshiped his image. These two were cast alive into the lake of fire burning with brimstone. [21] And the rest were killed with the sword which proceeded from the mouth of Him who sat on the horse. And all the birds were filled with their flesh.

---

3. John first saw the door of heaven opened when the church entered into it at the Rapture. Now it is opened a second time so the saints can return to earth to accompany their Lord. Jesus is here seen as riding a white horse (representing conquest) and bearing the name "Faithful and True" (in contrast to the forces of the Antichrist with their empty promises and lies). What other depictions of Jesus and the saints are mentioned (see verses 11–16)?

_____

_____

_____

_____

_____

_____

_____

4. The angel "standing in the sun" describes the vengeance that Christ will soon unleash by relating how the fowls of heaven will devour the flesh of the foes of heaven. This is the second supper depicted in this chapter—the "supper of the great God." What does John immediately see after this proclamation from the angel (see verses 17–21)?

_____

_____

_____

_____

The Thousand-Year Kingdom (Revelation 20:1–6)

¹ Then I saw an angel coming down from heaven, having the key to the bottomless pit and a great chain in his hand. ² He laid hold of the dragon, that serpent of old, who is the Devil and Satan, and bound him for a thousand years; ³ and he cast him into the bottomless pit, and shut him up, and set a seal on him, so that he should deceive the nations no more till the thousand years were finished. But after these things he must be released for a little while.

⁴ And I saw thrones, and they sat on them, and judgment was committed to them. Then I saw the souls of those who had been beheaded for their witness to Jesus and for the word of God, who had not worshiped the beast or his image, and had not received his mark on their foreheads or on their hands. And they lived and reigned with Christ for a thousand years. ⁵ But the rest of the dead did not live again until the thousand years were finished. This is the first resurrection. ⁶ Blessed and holy is he who has part in the first resurrection. Over such the second death has no power, but they shall be priests of God and of Christ, and shall reign with Him a thousand years.

5. The final conflict between the forces of Christ and the Antichrist is commonly referred to as "Armageddon." In Hebrew, this translates to _har megiddon_, the "mountain of Megiddo." Since there is no "Mount Megiddo" mentioned in Scripture, this could refer to the nearby Mount Carmel. This battle will result in the Antichrist and the false prophet being thrown into the lake of fire. What then happens to Satan, the dragon (see verses 1–3)?

_____

_____

_____

_____

6. The thousand-year reign of Christ on earth noted in this passage is commonly referred to as the "Millennial Kingdom." While John gives us no picture of what daily life will be like during this time on earth, we can be sure it will be one of peace, prosperity, purity, perpetual health, and personal joy. It will also be a time of *resurrection*. Who will be raised to life in the first resurrection? When will the second resurrection take place (see verses 4–6)?

_____

_____

_____

_____

The Final Judgment of Satan (Revelation 20:7–15)

[7] Now when the thousand years have expired, Satan will be released from his prison [8] and will go out to deceive the nations which are in the four corners of the earth, Gog and Magog, to gather them together to battle, whose number is as the sand of the sea. [9] They went up on the breadth of the earth and surrounded the camp of the saints and the beloved city. And fire came down from God out of heaven and devoured them. [10] The devil, who deceived them, was cast into the lake of fire and brimstone where the beast and the false prophet are. And they will be tormented day and night forever and ever.

[11] Then I saw a great white throne and Him who sat on it, from whose face the earth and the heaven fled away. And there was found no place for them. [12] And I saw the dead, small and great, standing

before God, and books were opened. And another book was opened, which is the Book of Life. And the dead were judged according to their works, by the things which were written in the books. [13] The sea gave up the dead who were in it, and Death and Hades delivered up the dead who were in them. And they were judged, each one according to his works. [14] Then Death and Hades were cast into the lake of fire. This is the second death. [15] And anyone not found written in the Book of Life was cast into the lake of fire.

---

7. When Satan is released after the thousand years have ended, he will be able to organize a rebellion of people who experienced the reign of Christ on earth. This final revolt will conclusively demonstrate that apart from God's intervention, humans are incapable of righteousness on their own. How will their rebellion end (see verses 7–10)?

_____

_____

_____

8. The final event to take place before the heavens and earth are made new is the Great White Throne Judgment. This event represents the final judgment against those who have refused to accept God's salvation through Christ. Those who reject God's salvation have, in a sense, demanded to be judged by their own works, and now that will happen. What will be the end result of their decision (see verses 11–14)?

_____

_____

_____

REVIEWING THE STORY

As heaven exalts over the fall of Babylon, two starkly different suppers take place. The first is the Marriage Supper of the Lamb, in which Christ takes His bride, the church. The second is the supper of the great God, during which the birds will feast on the bodies of those who die in the coming battle of Armageddon. Jesus and the saints of heaven will then return to earth, capture the beast (Antichrist) and false prophet, and cast them both into the lake of fire. The dragon (Satan) will be cast into the bottomless pit, and Jesus will reign on the earth with His saints for one thousand years. After this time, the dragon will be released and will raise up another army to do battle against Christ. But this force will again be defeated, after which time the dragon will also be cast into the lake of fire. Finally, those who have rejected Christ will be judged at the Great White Throne and also be sentenced to eternity in the lake of fire.

9. How is the bride of Christ arrayed for the wedding feast (see Revelation 19:8)?

_____

_____

_____

10. What happens at the supper of the great God (see Revelation 19:17–18)?

_____

_____

_____

11. For how long will Satan be bound when Jesus returns to earth (see Revelation 20:3)?

_____

_____

_____

12. How will those who refused Christ ultimately be judged (see Revelation 20:13)?

_____

_____

_____

_____

APPLYING THE MESSAGE

13. What is one aspect of God's character that compels you to offer Him praise?

_____

_____

_____

_____

14. How do you respond when you read about Satan's ultimate demise?

_____

_____

_____

_____

REFLECTING ON THE MEANING

In this section of Revelation, the apostle John reveals the events that will take place at what is known as the Great White Throne Judgment. This episode represents the final bar of justice in God's plan for the unsaved inhabitants of this world. Unlike earthly courtrooms, there will be a Judge but no jury, a prosecutor but no defender, and a sentence but no appeal. It is the place where sinners will stand before a holy God to give an account of their sins. There is no more awesome scene presented to us in the Word of God in terms of its significance.

It is important to remember the Great White Throne Judgment is *different* from the Judgment Seat of Christ. These two judgments bring into focus two different resurrections that will take place. Starting with Christ's resurrection from the grave, the *first resurrection* includes the saved dead of this age who are raised at the Rapture, those who are to be martyred during the Tribulation, and Old Testament saints who are raised at the end of the Tribulation. All this is incorporated into the first resurrection—the resurrection unto life.

The *second resurrection* will take place at the end of the Millennium Kingdom and will include "the rest of the dead [who] did not live again until the thousand years were finished" (Revelation 20:5). This resurrection takes place a thousand years after the first resurrection and includes those dead spiritually as well as physically. This is the resurrection that leads to the Great White Throne Judgment—at which there will be no believers in Christ.

The Judge on the Great White Throne will be none other than Jesus Himself. In the book of Acts, the disciple Peter declared that "[Christ] . . . was ordained by God to be Judge of the living and the dead" (Acts 10:42). So it is that Jesus will judge the spiritually *living* at the Judgment Seat of Christ and the spiritually *dead* at the Great White Throne. The One upon the throne will be the very One who gave His life for the redemption of those He is about to judge! He must therefore reject those who rejected Him and His plan for their salvation.

The concept of a final judgment and eternal punishment is not a popular doctrine in today's world—but it is one that is clearly spelled out in Scripture. In fact, Jesus spoke *three words* about hell for every *one word* that He spoke about heaven. It was His compassion that prompted Him to warn people of the punishment to come—and it should be our compassion that motivates us to warn them as well. It is our responsibility as believers to tell everyone about the salvation that Jesus offers.

JOURNALING YOUR RESPONSE

What is one practical way that you can take up this challenge to share about God's salvation?

THE NEW WORLD

Revelation 21:1–22:21

GETTING STARTED

What do you most want God to renew and restore in your life?

_____

_____

_____

_____

_____

_____

_____

_____

_____

_____

SETTING THE STAGE

As we come to the final chapters in Revelation, we find that the global purposes of God have been fulfilled. The rebellion of angels and the humans they inspired is finished, and they have been consigned to the lake of fire. Jesus Christ, the King of Kings and Lord of Lords, is on His throne and has begun His eternal reign. Sin has been replaced by righteousness. The redeemed are in glory with the Lamb. Every good and perfect promise of God has been realized.

All that remains, now that the heavy cloud of judgment has been lifted, is for John to describe the inheritance that God's people will receive. The final two chapters of Revelation are thus filled with good news for followers of Christ. In fact, many scholars believe that heaven is a continuation and perpetuation of the heavenly city that John describes in this portion of his vision, so studying that beautiful city will give us our first look at our eternal home with God.

Heaven is going to be a reality for us beyond all our human expectations. It will be a place where there will be no more pain, no more weeping, and no more death. When we look at the grand story of the Bible, we find that God always intended for us to dwell in the presence of the Father, Son, and Holy Spirit. This was His plan from the beginning of creation, before Adam and Eve sinned in the Garden of Eden and brought about all of the negative consequences that we experience today. There *will* be a new heaven, a new earth, and a new Jerusalem.

The final chapters in Revelation introduce us to all these "new" things the Father has prepared for those who love Him. The old things will pass away . . . and all things will be made *new*. Surprisingly, the Bible does not tell us much more than that about the establishment of this new heaven and earth! We know it will follow the Great White Throne Judgment and will be a renovation of this present heaven and earth by fire. But even though we do not have all the details, we can be certain it will be a wonderful place. We will finally and forever be in the presence of our heavenly Father . . . just as He always intended for us to be.

EXPLORING THE TEXT

All Things Made New (Revelation 21:1–11)

¹ Now I saw a new heaven and a new earth, for the first heaven and the first earth had passed away. Also there was no more sea. ² Then I,

John, saw the holy city, New Jerusalem, coming down out of heaven from God, prepared as a bride adorned for her husband. ³ And I heard a loud voice from heaven saying, "Behold, the tabernacle of God is with men, and He will dwell with them, and they shall be His people. God Himself will be with them and be their God. ⁴ And God will wipe away every tear from their eyes; there shall be no more death, nor sorrow, nor crying. There shall be no more pain, for the former things have passed away."

⁵ Then He who sat on the throne said, "Behold, I make all things new." And He said to me, "Write, for these words are true and faithful."

⁶ And He said to me, "It is done! I am the Alpha and the Omega, the Beginning and the End. I will give of the fountain of the water of life freely to him who thirsts. ⁷ He who overcomes shall inherit all things, and I will be his God and he shall be My son. ⁸ But the cowardly, unbelieving, abominable, murderers, sexually immoral, sorcerers, idolaters, and all liars shall have their part in the lake which burns with fire and brimstone, which is the second death."

⁹ Then one of the seven angels who had the seven bowls filled with the seven last plagues came to me and talked with me, saying, "Come, I will show you the bride, the Lamb's wife." ¹⁰ And he carried me away in the Spirit to a great and high mountain, and showed me the great city, the holy Jerusalem, descending out of heaven from God, ¹¹ having the glory of God. Her light was like a most precious stone, like a jasper stone, clear as crystal.

---

1. God originally created the earth to be the permanent home for human beings. However, when sin entered into the picture, the world became enemy-occupied territory. Ever since that time, God has been at work to reverse this situation and liberate the earth from its bondage to sin. In this section of Revelation, we see that liberation is now complete, as God institutes a new heaven, new earth, and new holy city of Jerusalem. What does John say will be absent from that city? Why is that significant (see verses 1–5)?

_____

_____

_____

_____

2. Jesus reiterates this inheritance is available to *anyone* who "thirsts" and comes to Christ as the "fountain" of eternal life. Those who faithfully follow Him and overcome the enemy shall partake in the new heaven and new earth. Immediately after John hears these words, he is whisked away by an angel for a closer look at the eternal dwelling place of all believers. How does John describe what this new city will be like (see verses 6–13)?

_____

_____

_____

_____

The Glory of the New Jerusalem (Revelation 21:12–27)

¹² Also she had a great and high wall with twelve gates, and twelve angels at the gates, and names written on them, which are the names of the twelve tribes of the children of Israel: ¹³ three gates on the east, three gates on the north, three gates on the south, and three gates on the west.

¹⁴ Now the wall of the city had twelve foundations, and on them were the names of the twelve apostles of the Lamb. ¹⁵ And he who talked with me had a gold reed to measure the city, its gates, and its wall. ¹⁶ The city is laid out as a square; its length is as great as its breadth. And he measured the city with the reed: twelve thousand furlongs. Its length, breadth, and height are equal. ¹⁷ Then

he measured its wall: one hundred and forty-four cubits, according to the measure of a man, that is, of an angel. [18] The construction of its wall was of jasper; and the city was pure gold, like clear glass. [19] The foundations of the wall of the city were adorned with all kinds of precious stones: the first foundation was jasper, the second sapphire, the third chalcedony, the fourth emerald, [20] the fifth sardonyx, the sixth sardius, the seventh chrysolite, the eighth beryl, the ninth topaz, the tenth chrysoprase, the eleventh jacinth, and the twelfth amethyst. [21] The twelve gates were twelve pearls: each individual gate was of one pearl. And the street of the city was pure gold, like transparent glass.

[22] But I saw no temple in it, for the Lord God Almighty and the Lamb are its temple. [23] The city had no need of the sun or of the moon to shine in it, for the glory of God illuminated it. The Lamb is its light. [24] And the nations of those who are saved shall walk in its light, and the kings of the earth bring their glory and honor into it. [25] Its gates shall not be shut at all by day (there shall be no night there). [26] And they shall bring the glory and the honor of the nations into it. [27] But there shall by no means enter it anything that defiles, or causes an abomination or a lie, but only those who are written in the Lamb's Book of Life.

---

3. John notes the New Jerusalem will have twelve gates, with the names of the twelve tribes written on them. The wall will have twelve foundations, with the names of the twelve apostles written on them. In this way, the city will represent the eternal home of God's people across all the ages. What else is unique about the composition of the walls? What is unique about its gates and its streets (see verses 12–21)?

4. The city will have no temple and no need of the sun or moon to illuminate it—not because these things have been *removed*, but because they been *expanded*. Where do we find the temple in the New Jerusalem? What will serve as its light (see verses 22–27)?

_____

_____

_____

_____

The River of Life (Revelation 22:1–11)

¹ And he showed me a pure river of water of life, clear as crystal, proceeding from the throne of God and of the Lamb. ² In the middle of its street, and on either side of the river, was the tree of life, which bore twelve fruits, each tree yielding its fruit every month. The leaves of the tree were for the healing of the nations. ³ And there shall be no more curse, but the throne of God and of the Lamb shall be in it, and His servants shall serve Him. ⁴ They shall see His face, and His name shall be on their foreheads. ⁵ There shall be no night there: They need no lamp nor light of the sun, for the Lord God gives them light. And they shall reign forever and ever.

⁶ Then he said to me, "These words are faithful and true." And the Lord God of the holy prophets sent His angel to show His servants the things which must shortly take place.

⁷ "Behold, I am coming quickly! Blessed is he who keeps the words of the prophecy of this book."

⁸ Now I, John, saw and heard these things. And when I heard and saw, I fell down to worship before the feet of the angel who showed me these things.

⁹ Then he said to me, "See that you do not do that. For I am your fellow servant, and of your brethren the prophets, and of those who keep the words of this book. Worship God." ¹⁰ And he said to me, "Do not seal the words of the prophecy of this book, for the time is

at hand. ¹¹ He who is unjust, let him be unjust still; he who is filthy, let him be filthy still; he who is righteous, let him be righteous still; he who is holy, let him be holy still."

---

5. John's concluding description of the New Jerusalem contains many parallels to the description of God's perfect creation that we find in the opening chapters of Genesis. Just as there was a river in Eden to provide life to the garden (see Genesis 2:10), so there is a river that proceeds from God's throne to provide life. Just as there was a tree of life in Eden (see 2:9), so there is a tree of life in the New Jerusalem—but this time, there are no restrictions to partaking of its fruit. What else will be different in the New Jerusalem? What roles will all of God's followers have in that place (see Revelation 22:1–5)?

_____

_____

_____

_____

6. The Bible relates that when the prophet Daniel received his vision, the angel instructed him to "seal the book until the time of the end" (Daniel 12:4). Why do you think John here is told *not* to seal the words of this prophetic vision (see Revelation 22:9–11)?

_____

_____

_____

_____

Jesus Testifies to the Churches (Revelation 22:12–21)

¹² "And behold, I am coming quickly, and My reward is with Me, to give to every one according to his work. ¹³ I am the Alpha and the Omega, the Beginning and the End, the First and the Last."

¹⁴ Blessed are those who do His commandments, that they may have the right to the tree of life, and may enter through the gates into the city. ¹⁵ But outside are dogs and sorcerers and sexually immoral and murderers and idolaters, and whoever loves and practices a lie.

¹⁶ "I, Jesus, have sent My angel to testify to you these things in the churches. I am the Root and the Offspring of David, the Bright and Morning Star."

¹⁷ And the Spirit and the bride say, "Come!" And let him who hears say, "Come!" And let him who thirsts come. Whoever desires, let him take the water of life freely.

¹⁸ For I testify to everyone who hears the words of the prophecy of this book: If anyone adds to these things, God will add to him the plagues that are written in this book; ¹⁹ and if anyone takes away from the words of the book of this prophecy, God shall take away his part from the Book of Life, from the holy city, and from the things which are written in this book.

²⁰ He who testifies to these things says, "Surely I am coming quickly."

Amen. Even so, come, Lord Jesus!

²¹ The grace of our Lord Jesus Christ be with you all. Amen.

---

7. John closes the book of Revelation with a reminder to his readers that Jesus has promised to return to this world and reward those who faithfully follow after Him. What does he reiterate is necessary on their part to receive God's blessings and rewards? Who does John say will be left "outside" the gates of the New Jerusalem (see verses 12–15)?

8. Jesus authenticates the message of Revelation with the words, "I, Jesus, have sent My angel to testify to you these things" (verse 16). What warning does He give to anyone who would seek to add to, alter, or take away from its prophecies (see verses 18–19)?

_____

_____

_____

_____

REVIEWING THE STORY

John's vision concludes with a glimpse of the new heaven and earth that God will establish for His people. The sea—the source of the beast—will be gone. There will also be no tabernacle, for the Lord will directly dwell with His people. The new earth will be free from the curse of sin, sickness, and death, and it will be available to all who receive salvation through Christ. John then sees the New Jerusalem descend from heaven. The city and its twelve walls are constructed of many precious jewels, and its streets are made of pure gold. The city has no need of a sun, for the Lord God and the Lamb provide its light. A pure river, consisting of the water of life, flows out from God's throne. In the middle of the city are trees of life, and all are now invited to partake of their fruit. John concludes with a reminder that Jesus has promised to return to this earth and will reward all those who overcome and faithfully serve Him.

9. What metaphor does John use to describe the New Jerusalem (see Revelation 21:3)?

_____

_____

_____

_____

10. What does the angel measure with the gold reed
(see Revelation 21:15)?

_____

_____

_____

11. What purpose does the tree of life serve in the New Jerusalem
(see Revelation 22:2)?

_____

_____

_____

12. What are Jesus' final words to His followers (see Revelation 22:20)?

_____

_____

_____

APPLYING THE MESSAGE

13. What does it mean to you that one day God will wipe every tear
from your eyes?

_____

_____

14. What does the grace of the Lord Jesus Christ look like in your life?

_____

_____

_____

REFLECTING ON THE MEANING

In the final chapters of Revelation, the apostle John answers the all-important question, "How should we live until the Rapture of the church takes place?" The answer to this question is essential to all of us who seek to follow Christ, because it must provide the framework for how we lead our lives. John's answer can be summarized in five short instructions.

First, we should walk submissively. Jesus tells John, "Blessed is he who keeps the words of the prophecy of this book" (Revelation 22:7). The word *keep* in this context means "to be submissive to." *Reading* God's Word is not enough. *Understanding* His prophecies is not enough. We must give God's Word authority in our lives. We discover His will and obey it.

Second, we should worship triumphantly. When John heard that Jesus was coming soon, he "fell down to worship" (verse 8). This should be our reaction, and we should use the worship of heaven as our guide. Heavenly worship focuses on the attributes and actions of God—who He is and what He has done. It never loses sight of the fact that God is in control. His purposes will be carried out and brought to completion. Those truths should guide our worship.

Third, we should work fervently. Jesus states that He will provide His reward "to every one according to his work" (verse 12). At the Judgment Seat of Christ, we will stand before the Lord as His gaze penetrates the innermost parts of our hearts and minds. The works we have done on His behalf will be evaluated as to kind, motive, and results. For this reason, to receive the rewards that God wants to give us, we must work and serve Him faithfully.

Fourth, we should witness urgently. John reminds his readers that those who follow Jesus will not be denied access to the holy city, but those who follow their own ways will be left outside its gates (see verses 14–15). This reality should compel us to share the gospel with anyone who needs to hear it. God's Word changes people's lives, and when people understand the coming judgments, they may be motivated to run to Christ.

Fifth, we should watch expectantly. Jesus' closing words to the apostle John reiterate His promise, "Surely I am coming quickly" (verse 20). The Rapture will occur so quickly that *no one* will have the chance to do last-minute spiritual work or make a last-minute eternal decision. Now is the time for all believers to open their eyes and begin watching expectantly for Jesus' return.

In one commentary on Revelation, the author paints a picture of a maiden whose beloved has gone on a voyage across the sea. She builds a signal fire each night in anticipation of his ship's return . . . until he comes to her. We are like that maiden, ever committed to the return of our Beloved. We live as signal lights for Him in a dark world—walking, worshipping, witnessing, working, and watching—until at last we witness His return.

JOURNALING YOUR RESPONSE

What do *you* want to be found doing when the Rapture occurs?

LEADER'S GUIDE

Thank you for choosing to lead your group through this study from Dr. David Jeremiah on *The Revelation of Jesus Christ*. Being a group leader has its own rewards, and it is our prayer that your walk with the Lord will deepen through this experience. During the twelve lessons in this study, you and your group will read passages from Revelation, explore key themes in the book based on teachings from Dr. Jeremiah, and review questions that will encourage group discussion. There are multiple components in this section that can help you structure your lessons and discussion time, so please be sure to read and consider each one.

BEFORE YOU BEGIN

Before your first meeting, make sure you and your group are well versed with the content of the lesson. Group members should have their own copy of *The Revelation of Jesus Christ* study guide prior to the first meeting so they can follow along and record their answers, thoughts, and insights. After the first week, you may wish to assign the study guide lesson as homework prior to the group meeting and then use the meeting time to discuss the content in the lesson.

To ensure everyone has a chance to participate in the discussion, the ideal size for a group is around eight to ten people. If there are more than ten people, break up the bigger group into smaller subgroups. Make sure the members are committed to participating each week, as this will help create stability and help you better prepare the structure of the meeting.

At the beginning of each week's study, start with the opening Getting Started question to introduce the topic you will be discussing. The members should answer briefly, as the goal is just for them to have an idea of the subject in their minds as you go over the lesson. This will allow the members to become engaged and ready to interact with the rest of the group.

After reviewing the lesson, try to initiate a free-flowing discussion. Invite group members to bring questions and insights they may have discovered to the next meeting, especially if they were unsure of the meaning of some parts of the lesson. Be prepared to discuss how biblical truth applies to the world we live in today.

WEEKLY PREPARATION

As the group leader, here are a few things that you can do to prepare for each meeting:

- *Be thoroughly familiar with the material in the lesson*. Make sure that you understand the content of each lesson so you know how to structure the group time and are prepared to lead the group discussion.

- *Decide, ahead of time, which questions you want to discuss*. Depending on how much time you have each week, you may not be able to reflect on every question. Select specific questions that you feel will evoke the best discussion.

- *Take prayer requests*. At the end of your discussion, take prayer requests from your group members and then pray for one another.

STRUCTURING THE DISCUSSION TIME

There are several ways to structure the duration of the study. You can choose to cover each lesson individually, for a total of twelve weeks of group meetings, or you can combine two lessons together per week, for a total of six weeks of group meetings. The following charts illustrate these options:

TWELVE-WEEK FORMAT

Week	Lessons Covered	Reading
1	A Vision in Exile	*Revelation 1:1–20*
2	Letters to Seven Churches	*Revelation 2:1–3:22*
3	A Glimpse of Heaven	*Revelation 4:1–5:14*
4	The Seal Judgments	*Revelation 6:1–7:17*
5	The Trumpet Judgments	*Revelation 8:1–9:21*
6	The Two Witnesses	*Revelation 10:1–11:19*
7	The Unholy Trinity	*Revelation 12:1–13:18*
8	Angelic Announcements	*Revelation 14:1–20*
9	The Bowl Judgments	*Revelation 15:1–16:21*
10	Babylon Falls	*Revelation 17:1–18:24*
11	Satan Is Defeated	*Revelation 19:1–20:15*
12	The New World	*Revelation 21:1–22:21*

SIX-WEEK FORMAT

Week	Lessons Covered	Reading
1	A Vision in Exile / Letters to Seven Churches	*Revelation 1:1–3:22*
2	A Glimpse of Heaven / The Seal Judgments	*Revelation 4:1–7:17*
3	The Trumpet Judgments / The Two Witnesses	*Revelation 8:1–11:19*
4	The Unholy Trinity / Angelic Announcements	*Revelation 12:1–14:20*
5	The Bowl Judgments / Babylon Falls	*Revelation 15:1–18:24*
6	Satan Is Defeated / The New World	*Revelation 19:1–22:21*

In regard to organizing your time when planning your group Bible study, the following two schedules, for sixty minutes and ninety minutes, can give you a structure for the lesson:

Section	60 Minutes	90 Minutes
Welcome: Members arrive and get settled	5 minutes	10 minutes
Getting Started Question: Prepares the group for interacting with one another	10 minutes	10 minutes
Message: Review the lesson	15 minutes	25 minutes
Discussion: Discuss questions in the lesson	25 minutes	35 minutes
Review and Prayer: Review the key points of the lesson and have a closing time of prayer	5 minutes	10 minutes

As the group leader, it is up to you to keep track of the time and keep things moving according to your schedule. If your group is having a good discussion, don't feel the need to stop and move on to the next question. Remember, the purpose is to pull together ideas and share unique insights on the lesson. Encourage everyone to participate, but don't be concerned if certain group members are more quiet. They may just be internally reflecting on the questions and need time to process their ideas before they can share them.

GROUP DYNAMICS

Leading a group study can be a rewarding experience for you and your group members—but that doesn't mean there won't be challenges. Certain members may feel uncomfortable discussing topics that they consider very personal and might be afraid of being called on. Some members might have disagreements on specific issues. To help prevent these scenarios, consider the following ground rules:

- If someone has a question that may seem off topic, suggest that it be discussed at another time, or ask the group if they are okay with addressing that topic.

- If someone asks a question you don't know the answer to, confess that you don't know and move on. If you feel comfortable, invite other group members to give their opinions or share their comments based on personal experience.
- If you feel like a couple of people are talking much more than others, direct questions to people who may not have shared yet. You could even ask the more dominating members to help draw out the quiet ones.
- When there is a disagreement, encourage the group members to process the matter in love. Invite members from opposing sides to evaluate their opinions and consider the ideas of the other members. Lead the group through Scripture that addresses the topic, and look for common ground.

When issues arise, encourage your group to think of Scripture: "Love one another" (John 13:34), "If it is possible, as much as it depends on you, live peaceably with all men" (Romans 12:18), and, "Be swift to hear, slow to speak, slow to wrath" (James 1:19).

ABOUT

Dr. David Jeremiah and Turning Point

Dr. David Jeremiah is the founder of Turning Point, a ministry committed to providing Christians with sound Bible teaching relevant to today's changing times through radio and television broadcasts, audio series, books, and live events. Dr. Jeremiah's teaching on topics such as family, prayer, worship, angels, and biblical prophecy forms the foundation of Turning Point.

David and his wife, Donna, reside in El Cajon, California, where he serves as the senior pastor of Shadow Mountain Community Church. David and Donna have four children and twelve grandchildren.

In 1982, Dr. Jeremiah brought the same solid teaching to San Diego television that he shares weekly with his congregation. Shortly thereafter, Turning Point expanded its ministry to radio. Dr. Jeremiah's inspiring messages can now be heard worldwide on radio, television, and the internet.

Because Dr. Jeremiah desires to know his listening audience, he travels nationwide holding ministry rallies and spiritual enrichment conferences that touch the hearts and lives of many people. According to Dr. Jeremiah, "At some point in time, everyone reaches a turning point; and for every person, that moment is unique, an experience to hold onto forever. There's so much changing in today's world that sometimes it's difficult to choose the right path. Turning Point offers people an understanding of God's Word and seeks to make a difference in their lives."

Dr. Jeremiah has authored numerous books, including *Escape the Coming Night* (Revelation), *The Handwriting on the Wall* (Daniel), *What in the World Is Going On?*, *The Coming Economic Armageddon*, *I Never Thought I'd See the Day!*, *God Loves You: He Always Has—He Always Will*, *Agents of the Apocalypse*, *Agents of Babylon*, *Revealing the Mysteries of Heaven*, *People Are Asking . . . Is This the End?*, *A Life Beyond Amazing*, *Overcomer*, *The Book of Signs*, *Everything You Need*, *Forward*, and *Where Do We Go from Here?*

New Bible Study Series
from Dr. David Jeremiah

The Jeremiah Bible Study Series captures Dr. David Jeremiah's forty-plus years of commitment to teaching the whole Word of God. Each volume contains twelve lessons for individuals and groups to explore what the Bible says, what it meant to the people at the time it was written, and what it means to us today. Out of his lifelong ministry of *delivering the unchanging Word of God to an ever-changing world*, Dr. Jeremiah has written this Bible-strong study series focused not on causes, current events, or politics, but on the solid truth of Scripture.

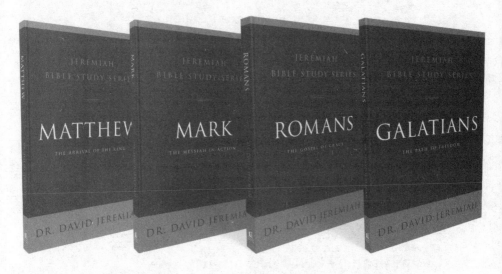

9780310091493	Matthew	9780310091707	Philippians
9780310091516	Mark	9780310091721	Colossians and Philemon
9780310091530	Luke	9780310091745	1 & 2 Thessalonians
9780310091554	John	9780310091769	1 & 2 Timothy and Titus
9780310091608	Acts	9780310091783	Hebrews
9780310091622	Romans	9780310091806	James
9780310091646	1 Corinthians	9780310091844	1, 2, 3 John and Jude
9780310097488	2 Corinthians	9780310091820	1 & 2 Peter
9780310091660	Galatians	9780310091868	Revelation
9780310091684	Ephesians		

Available now at your favorite bookstore.